An Investigation of Psychotherapists' Experiences In Relation To Ubuntu

by

LUMKA SYBIL QANGULE

ABSTRACT

Psychotherapy is a Eurocentric concept and practice that has migrated to South Africa with technology, as part of the general transfer of knowledge (Mkhize, 2003). It has embedded Eurocentric principles that sometimes do not easily accommodate working with Africans. It has been practised by psychotherapists of African origin with clients of African origin, but is based upon Eurocentric ideas and guidelines for practice. Many African people consider their core values to be uBuntu, rooted in a principle '*umntu ngumntu ngabantu*' (translated as 'a human being is a human being because of other human beings'). Some important features of uBuntu are interdependence, respect, spirituality and the primacy of communality as an approach to life. Some of the ways in which these impact on daily functioning are not foregrounded by adherence to Western principles. The use of only Eurocentric principles when working with clients of African origin may thus not lead to the desired outcomes in psychotherapy. However, these Eurocentric principles are recognised and enforced by the authoritative bodies in the field of psychology, such as the Health Professions Council of South Africa. A distinction will be made between the more inflexible ethical principles of psychology and the ideas of therapy frames. Therapy frames are not seen as being as rigid as ethical codes and they could be augmented, to be appropriate for the context, particularly in the commonly multicultural settings that are found here.

Psychotherapists of African origin are torn between abiding by the ethical principles that they have been taught and practising in the way that they, together with their clients, have been socialised. Abiding by the principles as described in the codes is safe because it does not pose any threat of being sanctioned by the regulator of practice, but clients may be let down and there may be limited success with certain clients. This clash of ideas of ways of practice poses dissonance and many dilemmas among psychotherapists of African origin.

Due to the nature of this study, Interpretative Phenomenological Analysis (IPA) was adopted as a suitable methodology, where eight practising amaXhosa psychotherapists were interviewed about their experiences of incorporating uBuntu in their psychotherapy practice. The raw data from initial interviews were analysed and the findings concluded that although psychotherapists were trained in Western ways of practice, they included some practices of uBuntu in their practice as well as upholding some Eurocentric principles that seemed to be helpful for their clientele. Subsequently a summary of the findings were discussed with participants in a focus group setting, where participants endorsed and expanded upon their original responses.

With the above in mind, a psychotherapy model called uBuntu -Centred Psychotherapy was created, which reflects the principles and therapy frames that have been found to be useful in treating clients of African origin. This modality is more congruent with the worldviews and style of living of many South Africans, in the post-apartheid era. It embraces some Eurocentric principles that are relevant for Africans, while it is embedded in the phenomena and way of life reflected in uBuntu, a predominant mode of functioning for the group that was the focus of this study, the amaXhosa. The study ends by making recommendations for practice, as well as highlighting the need for further and more extensive research to contribute to the project of Africanising psychotherapy.

Contents

List of Tables

List of Figures

List of Abbreviations

CEU	Continuing Education Units
CPD	Continuing Professional Development
DSM	Diagnostic and Statistical Manual for Mental Disorders
HIV/AIDS	Human Immunodeficiency Virus/ Acquired Immune Deficiency Syndrome
HPCSA	Health Professions Council of SA
IPA	Interpretative Phenomenological Analysis
MDD	Major Depressive Disorder
NTU	African root word that points to the causative force, godliness, being-ness, life force, community and essence, and that acts as a sign of *universal resemblance*
SA	South Africa
WEIRD	Western, Educated, Industrialised, Rich and Democratic

CHAPTER 1

INTRODUCTION TO THE STUDY

1.1 Introduction

This study is conducted in the field of psychology, particularly psychotherapy; which is conducted by qualified psychologists who are registered in Health Professions Council of SA (HPCSA). People find psychotherapy helpful, in that in individual psychotherapy they deal with interpersonal life problems (Smith, Strumpher & Morton, 2015). However in South Africa (SA), the success of psychotherapy is susceptible to different culturally influenced worldview clashes that are caused by the fact that psychotherapy originates from the developed world, the 'West', but it is practised among African people using Western principles. These traditional and Western worldview differences may bring about dissonance in amaXhosa practising psychotherapists. In this regard, Madu (2015) asserts that using appropriate psychotherapeutic values for modern African clients is a challenge to many psychotherapists treating Black Africans.

Schultz, Bahrami-Rad, Beauchamp and Henrich (2018) recently noted that psychological research has predominantly focused on the values and peculiarities of "Western, Educated, Industrialised, Rich and Democratic (WEIRD)" societies. This may conceal substantial global variations, since such societies represent only 12 percent of the world population, is not only unrepresentative of humans as a species, but they are outliers on many measures (Azar, 2010). The applications of psychology in psychotherapy have been a part of these developments, since the profession emerged from Europe; and has become a popular form of treatment in WEIRD settings. Utsey, Fischer and Belvet (2010, 182) note that traditional psychotherapy approaches and techniques "are culturally encapsulated in a Eurocentric theoretical framework and worldview". Leach, Aten, Boyer, Strain and Bradshaw (2010, 14) thus emphasise the need for psychotherapists to develop their awareness of the cultural influences, in which they have been immersed, "regardless of ethnic background" and that their cultural heritages are "comprised of multiple identities, which may influence work with clients (who also have multiple identities)". In this study, the terms 'Western' and 'Eurocentric' are used to denote these ideas.

Many Black psychotherapists may experience tensions between Western forms of psychotherapy (embedded with Western values), which in many cases do not properly address or appeal to the needs of African clients and African traditional forms of Psychotherapy, which have so far belonged to the exclusive domain of African traditional and religious faith healing practises and their values (Madu, 2015). In SA, psychologists are challenged to critically review their roles and professional identities, in order to ensure quality, accessibility and culturally appropriate services within a society that is characterised by racism and gender inequalities as well as violent conflict due to apartheid (Seedat, MacKenzie & Stevens, 2004). Moreover, Bojuwoye and Sodi (2010) indicate that Western psychological healthcare models have been found to be ineffective when applied to the differing contexts of other peoples.

I seek to find ways of practising psychotherapy that would assist psychotherapists to practice in an acceptable but effective manner without compromising people's ways of living but also respecting the working rules and ethics of psychology. Canter, Bennett, Jones and Nagy (1999) suggest that when a psychologist is confronted with ethical issues, and is uncertain about a course of action to take in a particular situation, that psychologist should consult others who are knowledgeable about ethical issues in order to choose a proper response. In my quest to find solutions to the challenges I have been experiencing in my practise, I have decided to undertake research to find out from other practising psychotherapists about their ways of practising psychotherapy that benefits my clients, hence this study.

I start by giving my personal motivations for conducting this study and then proceed to discuss the SA context. This is followed by the background to the problem, the statement of the problem, then the purpose of the study, and the research approach I follow in conducting this study. I then proceed to the significance of the study, thereafter I define some of the crucial concepts I use in this study. I finalise this chapter by overviewing this thesis.

1.2 Personal motivation for this study

My personal experiences as a counselling psychologist motivated me to carry out this study. I have been a counselling psychologist registered with Health Professions of SA (HPCSA) for over a decade. I am of amaXhosa origin, living in the Eastern Cape, SA. Most of my clients in my private practise are also amaXhosa. Most of them inform me that: "*Ndikhethe ukuza kuwe ngoba wena uthetha olulwimi lwam, uzoyiva kwaye uyiqonde kakuhle le nto*

ndiyithethayo" (I chose to come to you because you speak the same language as myself, you will hear and understand exactly what I want to say). My training is in Eurocentric ways of practising psychology; however I work among amaXhosa who have not studied psychology but express the need for services to deal with challenges to their mental health.
I find myself being torn between my culturally influenced traditions or ways of living and my training or what is expect of me by the psychology profession. I understand the way of living of my people because I also live amongst them but I have been trained to practise in a way that sometimes contradicts the way of living of my people. Sometimes I feel that by strictly complying with the expectations of Eurocentric psychology I am failing my amaXhosa clients because I use Western principles when working with them. At other times I go with the expectations of my client such as advice-giving, or accepting a gift and get apprehensive and uncomfortable and have thoughts such as, what am I doing? What am I doing if I get caught by the authorities (HPCSA)? Obviously the sorts of actions to which I refer are not harmful to me as a practitioner nor to my client. For example, a client would ask me for advice in a certain situation, I would ask from my client what he/she thinks should do, but the client would say I came to you for advice how can you ask what I think, tell me what I must do in this situation. I would further suggest options and ask clients to choose what they think they should do the client would say please choose for me. If I refuse completely to choose for my client, they get disappointed and feel failed by me as a practitioner. As umXhosa I understand that '*inyathi ibuzwa kwabaphambili*'(translated as you get advice/direction from the more knowledgeable people – you get direction from the people who have travelled the route before you). On the other hand if I eventually advised the client, the client would mostly be happy and feel that I have provided a service or met their expectations, but I would feel guilty because that is not how I should practise, according to my training.

I figured out that I am in this dilemma due to my tensions between my Western training and my practise, which is among my people. In other words, my culturally influenced perspective and my training appear to be in some conflict with each other. My training is a 'one size fits all' approach, but it does not fit me, I am looking for something more suitable for me. This experience poses challenges in my practise, since I find myself torn between accepting, thus acknowledging and appreciating my traditional worldview; as well as abiding by the ethical codes of Eurocentric psychotherapy. I believe that the dissonance I sometimes experience may be due to psychotherapy originating from a Western perspective and therefore having embedded Eurocentric principles, ethics and styles that do not necessarily accommodate other worldviews. In this regard, Van Dyk and Nefale (2003) indicate that imposing Western principles on African people might involve unnecessarily labelling of certain clients' experiences as pathological, based on conflicting models of explaining illness, health and healing. *Ukuthwasa* is an example, whereby an individual receives a divine calling from *izinyanya* (ancestors) to a higher service of healing to treat people as a *sangoma* (Ally & August, 2018) or divine healer. If the call is not accepted, the individual may experience the continued hearing of voices, visions and dreams or nightmares (Ally & August, 2018). Then there are *Amafufunyana*, which are culturally influenced conditions of amaZulu and amaXhosa, suggesting that an individual may be possessed by evil spirits, impacting on behaviour, speech and thoughts. The exclusion of such context-specific experiences in the dominant theoretical knowledge of psychology, may lead to the individual being incorrectly diagnosed according to diagnostic criteria as defined in the Diagnostic and Statistical Manual for Mental Disorders (DSM) with a very specific mental disorder or with a diagnosis clumped under the category 'culture-bound syndrome' (Ally & August, 2018).

Having the above in mind, in this study therefore I am trying to find out whether other amaXhosa psychologists are also experiencing similar dilemmas in their practises. If so, what can be done in order for us to practise comfortably, without noncompliance to principles of the HPCSA, to principles of the HPCSA, or having guilty feelings about failing our clients? These thoughts were all motivations for undertaking this study.

1.3 Context

In this section I discuss some contextual features that create the need for much broader applications of and access to psychotherapy. These relate to the specific province in which the study is located as well as relevant features of the broader national context.

This study takes place in the Eastern Cape Province, which is the largest province in SA, comprising the two former Bantustans of the Transkei and Ciskei, as well as a substantial amount of other land settled by farmers (Wilson, 2011). Most people that live in the former Bantustans are Black, to some degree illiterate and unemployed (Wilson, 2011). Comparing different settlements, Westaway (2012) notes that in the Eastern Cape Province of SA, people who live in Port Elizabeth, Makhanda and East London who are both Black and white, are mostly governed by rights, democracy and development while people who live in

Keiskammahoek, Cofimvaba and Lusikisiki, who happen to be all Black, are governed by custom, tradition and welfare.

Wilson (2011) explains that in SA there were good Black schools that were pioneered by the London Missionary Society and others, such as Lovedale, Healdtown and St Matthews in the Eastern Cape Province before the establishment of the apartheid regime. However, all these were replaced by Bantu education, which was designed to mould Black people for the bottom rungs of a racist political economic structure (Wilson, 2011). There were great discrepancies in the quality of education offered to children during apartheid times, depending on racial categories. Moreover, white teachers were paid considerably far more than equally qualified Black teachers (Wilson, 2011). As a result Black people were educated for being employed as semiskilled or unskilled labourers who become migrant labourers in the mines where they generated wealth for white mine owners, while they were generating poverty for themselves as Black mine workers (Wilson & Rampele, 1989). Westaway (2012) describes that since the Eastern Cape Province of SA was demarcated in 1994, the democratic government of the new SA has done little to shift the levels of poverty, unemployment and inequality, which it inherited from the apartheid regime. This is despite its best intentions and efforts to develop effective policies or despite the expectations of its voters.

Poverty is thus widespread in this province, particularly in the former Bantustans, with many households dependent on social welfare. In other words, government grants contribute substantially to the income of the poor because of high rate of unemployment (Westaway, 2012). Moreover, high rates of illiteracy, which led to people being employed in low income salary brackets, have also contributed to the poor economic status of the province. Even those who are educated among Blacks remain far behind in such subjects as mathematics; which were deliberately denied to African pupils during Bantu Education years (Wilson, 2011). Thus the legal and a social colour bar combined with blatant discrimination in human capital investment for 100 years and more has built a racial bias into the underlying pattern of income distribution that cannot be simply erased overnight (Wilson, 2011).

Westaway (2012) notes that most people living in the Eastern Cape Province survive below the poverty line. Furthermore, the provision of education, health, water and sanitation infrastructure and services has been distressingly inadequate. These harsh experiences affect the needs of the majority who still experience the sequelae of post-traumatic stress; and who have had their identities deeply affected by always feeling not good enough they then express their distress in violent behaviour, substance abuse, intimate partner violence, among others.

According to Lund, et al. (2018) increasing global evidence exists that mental disorders in populations are strongly socially determined. Social and economic conditions have a direct influence on the prevalence and severity of mental disorders in people; adverse social and economic circumstances including poverty, income inequality, interpersonal and collective violence and forced immigration are the key determinants of mental disorders. Nglazi, et al. (2016) indicates that SA is under-resourced regarding mental health services; which results in underdiagnoses and under-treatment of mental disorders. Moreover barriers to help-seeking and treatment for mental illnesses, include stigma, low health literacy levels and financial difficulties.

SA is characterised by an enormous and diverse burden of diseases and comorbidity of Major Depressive Disorder (MDD) including infectious diseases such as HIV/AIDS, high rates of violence and child illnesses. Flisher, et al. (2012) indicates that in SA HIV infection, substance use, and exposure to violence increases vulnerability to mental disorders. SA is faced with neuropsychiatric disorders given the high rates of unemployment and poverty, high rates of crime, inadequate social services and potentially stressful living conditions (Nglazi et al, 2016). Lund, Myer, Stein, Williams and Flisher (2013) add that low income increases the risk for mental disorders, through increased risk of adverse life events and reduced access to resources that can buffer the effects of those life events, which contribute to the social causation of mental illnesses. Furthermore, in low and middle income countries little is known about the connection between mental disorders and reduced income, in spite of the evidence of a substantial burden of mental illness and severely under-resourced mental health care systems.

Sibeko, et al. (2018) note that mental neurological and substance use disorders contribute significantly to the global burden of disease accounting for 21.2% of years lived with disability, despite mental services in general which are under-resourced. According to Sibeko, et al. (2018) in low resourced settings, the treatment gap (an indication of the proportion of individuals with mental illness who remain untreated in spite of the existence of effective treatments) is as high as 90%. According to Flisher et al. (2012) mental health problems in childhood and adolescence pose a major threat to public health. Petersen, Bhana and Swartz (2012) note that depression is estimated to become the second leading burden of illness globally by 2030. There is a growing recognition of the need to scale up treatment efforts for mental disorders in SA, suggested in the first National Summit on Mental Health held in April 2012 (Petersen, Bhana & Swartz, 2012).

With all of the above in mind, psychological intervention is needed. Seedat, MacKenzie and Stevens (2004) state that psychologists are called to cast aside the myth of political neutrality and the disempowering aspects of psychology, so as to emphasise the potential of psychology. De la Ray and Ipser (2004) note that many SA psychologists have debated how psychology could become more relevant to the local socio-political context. Among other things, this is due to the major factors responsible for the difficulties in applying Western healthcare, where these lenses mostly ignore culturally influenced realities of people in other contexts. Moreover, Western psychological practice relies heavily on natural science, ignoring the role of social conditions, power relations and societal institutional arrangements that shape people's conceptualisations of illness and help-seeking behaviours (Bojuwoye & Sodi, 2010).

The following table distinguishes predominant features of Western and African psychologies as derived from Nwoye (2015). It is important to note though that Nwoye is separating these aspects as if they are discontinuous, whereas it is a matter of the features that predominate or that have been evident. For example, his first point does not illustrate the recent dramatic increase in qualitative studies in psychology, which do not conform to this description.

Table 1.1: Predominant features of Western and African psychologies (Nwoye, 2015)

Western psychology	**African psychology**
Makes use of objective, quantitative measurement.	Makes use of viewing humans holistically and their existential contexts that are visible and tangible realities.
Focuses on material, measurable and observable terms.	Focus on human religions and spirituality which are important influences of humans.
What is observed?	Meaning of things to people.
Death of a body is a death of a mind as well.	Death of the body is not death of the mind and memory.

This current study is therefore being conducted in a province that has experienced neglect both during and after apartheid, where there are elevated levels of mental distress and social problems as a result of apartheid. In addition, many people in the province are immersed in cultural contexts where African worldviews predominate; thus they are likely to need psychological services that follow the principles identified by Nwoye (2015) as listed in the right-hand column of the table above.

1.4 Background to the problem

In recent years Africans and other non-Western therapists have been practicing psychotherapy using Western principles, ethics and styles with their people. Washington (2010) says since psychology emanated from the West, what is perceived as normal in the West is universally normalised. For African therapists, like me, this could be experienced as a dichotomy: being are born and raised in specific African ways of living, but trained in the Western worldview, yet having to practice psychotherapy with African people. In like manner, Nwoye (2015) asserts that Western (Eurocentric) psychology has been insensitive to the realities and challenges confronting African people. Eurocentric psychology has conceptualised a person in an individualistic way and does not give due importance to the influences of the society. Mkhize (2003) indicates that modern psychology was brought to developing countries as part of general transfer of knowledge from the West as well as technology. Some American and European research studies that have been conducted in Africa have proved to be disrespectful, misrepresentative and highly judgemental of the ways of living and peoples of Africa.

In some instances. African clients were labelled as pathological due to them being treated in European understanding of health and healing. This may lead to inaccurate judgements about inferiority in some instances or potential misinterpretation of the behaviour of Africans (Washington, 2010). It is due to the above mentioned facts that Amaeshi & Idemudia (2015) suggest that the current practice of Western psychotherapy in Africa be revised and that the concept of African or African-Centred Psychotherapy be pursued vigorously. That is to say a science that is oblivious of its culturally influenced environment condemns itself to irrelevance. For this reason, any form of psychotherapeutic practice without culturally influenced justification may be without substance and superficial.

It is important to realise that African influenced traditions put emphasis on kinship care, invisible loyalty to the guardianship of ancestral spirits, spirituality and the inter-connections between the natural and the spirit world (Striker, 1994). An African psychology therefore needs to incorporate such important elements. In this light, Mkhize (2003) suggests that the use of only Western principles in therapy may create some tensions and possibly confusion. A more holistic approach leads to African psychology that is about the whole being (Washington, 2010), meaning a holistic view of the actual person.

With this in mind, one of the major values of African people is uBuntu, as discussed in chapter 3. The uBuntu concept is aimed at incorporating the African traditional worldview into psychotherapy, thereby acknowledging the importance of this is a way of living on self as well as promoting mental health and rendered the necessary respect it deserves (Moodley & West, 2005). uBuntu thus determines how communities live and therefore define their identities. Moreover, to conduct psychotherapy sessions that do not embrace uBuntu while treating Africans, may fail some of African people (Van Dyk and Nefale, 2005; Muwanga-Zake, 2009).

African psychology is aimed at improving understandings of the contemporary African way of living (Nwoye, 2015). In other words, African psychology is mainly concerned with understanding the system of being-ness, the features of human functioning and restoration of natural order to human development. African psychology is rooted in the relational interdependence between individual and community, expressed as *umntu ngumntu ngabantu,* translated as "a human is human through humans" (Nwoye, 2015, 109).

To clarify, I am aware of Praeg (2014)'s argument that distinguishes between Ubuntu and ubuntu. uBuntu involves caring, sharing, respect, compassion and ensures a happy and qualitative human community life in the spirit of family, communality, oneness, cooperation and sharing. He perceives the former as a philosophical expression in the postcolonial retrodiction (to utilize present information or ideas to infer or explain the state of affairs), while the latter refers to living practise or unadulterated forms of African social life. As much as I appreciate this distinction, in isiXhosa *u* is a prefix of some nouns such as *ukutya* (food), *umntwana* (a child), *umlambo* (the river), which can be interpreted as 'the'. In this study, I chose to combine the philosophical element and the way of living of Africans by writing it as uBuntu. I also do not use italics when writing uBuntu because it is a word that is acceptable in SA English usage (Praeg & Magadla, 2014). Equally important, uBuntu is an African way of viewing the world, which a significant number of ethnic groups and individuals adhere to (Murithi, 2006).

In my practise I see mostly employed females rather than male clients. My clients have their psychotherapy sessions funded by medical aids and the predominant requests for assistance are for depression, marital challenges, financial problems, work related stresses among other things. It is clear that an increasing number of amaXhosa are consulting with psychotherapists. We therefore need a system that is responsive to that and treatment that is in line with the way of living of amaXhosa: a therapeutic framework that is informed by uBuntu. In this study I seek to find out how amaXhosa psychotherapists experience practising using Eurocentric psychotherapy principles while working with amaXhosa clients. I further seek to investigate what of uBuntu principles might be integrated into psychotherapy that can improve the current state of affairs, while treating amaXhosa clients.

1.5 Statement of the problem

Whilst in earlier times or in traditional living contexts, people might have sought assistance for mental distress from traditional healers or possibly religious sources, with rapidly increasing urbanisation, people are beginning to seek help from psychotherapy. They hear about psychology from employers, health practitioners and other community sources; so they then seek assistance.

While practising psychotherapy with amaXhosa clients using Western principles may bring about dissonance and confusion among psychotherapists, there seems to be no model of practice that accommodates Black psychotherapists, suiting their clients adequately. The gap in the knowledge is therefore a model of practice that incorporates uBuntu principles in psychotherapy. In other words, how can uBuntu as a way of living of amaXhosa be incorporated in to psychotherapy?

According to Moodley, Sutherland and Oulanova, (2008) there has been a growing trend in the West to seek alternative, complementary and traditional healing not only as a reaction to Western biomedicine but also to the mind set of bringing ideas into psychotherapy. As much as traditional healing aims to restore harmony and balance within the individual through a symbiosis of the body, mind and spirit, traditional healing practices, when compared to Western health care systems, are seen to be ‘‘worlds apart’’ with different models of illness and health, operating within a different worldview. It is critical for psychotherapists to understand different life styles that are influenced by various cultural contexts in order to appropriately understand the individual (Ally & August, 2018). As such, social relations, practices, ways of relating to each other and responding to life experiences are context specific and must be accommodated in psychotherapy practice (Moodley, et al, 2008).

Since 1994 psychotherapy services are still largely inaccessible and seemingly irrelevant to the majority despite endless pleas for relevance (De la Rey & Ipser, 2004). Ratele (2017) notes a need for recognition by psychologists in SA that we are not immune to calls for the decolonization of society, and encourages psychologists to seriously engage in these evolving conversations. Decolonisation, dialogue and engagement between scientific thinking and cultural beliefs are necessary, in order to challenge the perceived notion of African thinking as saturated in superstition, fantasy and backwardness (Ally & August, 2018). Decolonisation tackles the ways in which people have previously been discriminated against, whilst oppressed considering alternative worldviews that are more congruent with people's experiences; and also tackling the structural and institutional impacts that are the remains of a divisive colonial heritage. This study is therefore part of considering ways in which psychology might be decolonised and constructed to better suit the majority of people in SA.

1.6 The aim of the study

The aim of this study is to provide or add to knowledge concerning psychotherapists' experiences in their practice regarding the incorporation of principles of uBuntu. Moreover, it is designed to understand the lived experiences and dilemmas of psychotherapists who engage with uBuntu practices in their psychotherapy and interpret how participants make sense of such.

As an attempt to make psychology relevant to the majority of SA, the understanding these experiences and dilemmas will hopefully respond to the call for the decolonisation of higher education in SA. This will result in students, teachers, researchers, therapists developing more African psychology, to enable university courses, research, professional programmes, therapies, as well as networks (Ratele, 2017), to reflect African traditions of thought (Ally & August, 2018), in order to build a relevant, appropriate, socio-politically conscious, transformed discipline and profession (Ratele, 2017).

1.7 Research approach

This study takes a qualitative approach to research. In order to do justice in this study, an Interpretative Phenomenological Analysis (IPA) is followed because it seeks to investigate the lived experiences of psychotherapists regarding uBuntu in their psychotherapy practice. IPA is committed to examining how people make sense of their major life experiences.

Moreover, IPA researchers are particularly interested in the everyday ways of making meaning of lived experiences of key informants, particularly if something important has happened in their lives (Smith, Larkin & Flowers, 2009).

1.8 Significance of the study

As stated above, nowadays universities and scholars are concerned with decolonising Eurocentric-influenced curriculums (Le Grange, 2016). Psychology has been unduly influenced by Western approaches and it is timely to decolonise it so it is appropriate and inclusive of all the people in SA. The term "decolonization" is both an evocative and provocative term that leads people into spaces in which few psychologists authentically engage, because it is a complex debate about historical, epistemological, methodological, theoretical, ideological, philosophical, pedagogical, discursive, ethical and practical concerns (Pillay, 2016). Decolonization is useful in that it introduces a much more relevant psychology that dismantles oppressive postcolonial relations of power and calls for a specific psycho-political orientation of the profession.

Ally and August (2018) assert that discussions on the relevance of psychology in SA are expected to incorporate culturally influenced practices, belief systems and the implications for the lived experiences of individuals. However, these may bring about dissonance between scientific rationale and culturally influenced practices. The Africanising of curricula is associated with the perception that Western scientific thinking is absolute at the expense of cultural belief systems. Equally important is a racist resistance to Africanising the curriculum. Any theory developed outside of the boundaries of SA must be critically re-examined in terms of relevance and applicability and where necessary, the relevant theoretical changes must be made.

Ally and August (2018) note that a decolonised education will not be an instant reality despite its noble framing. The process involved in rethinking African thought is a complicated matter and forces both academics and students to grapple with realities that are outside of what they have come to learn and trust over years of education and training. Pillay (2016) asserts that even if psychology is resistant to change, the zeitgeist has forced decolonization onto the national agenda. This was evidenced by the student-led #Rhodes Must Fall and #Fees Must Fall movements, which were conversations critiquing the rainbow nation ideas and transformation discourses. In other words, these movements were replacing politics of hope and reconciliation with a politics of radical dissent and anger (Pillay, 2016).

It is therefore essential to identify and develop culturally appropriate avenues for clinical practice for practitioners who work with indigenous people (Kilcullen, Swinbourne & Cadet-James, 2018). Barnes and Siswana (2018) argue that although there are various contributions towards psychology and decolonisation; such contributions reveal the complexities of decolonisation that extend beyond the ideas that decolonisation means to replace one body of knowledge with another. These decolonisation contributions further demonstrate how critical movements can be mobilised under decolonisation in order to strengthen their cause as well as the loosening of the language and boundaries of psychological scholarship that could potentially improve the relevance of discipline. Thus in this study I intend to contribute knowledge within which a partially decolonised framework of psychotherapy is suggested.

1.9 Definitions of terms

In the following section I briefly introduce key concepts and constructs. These concepts are discussed in depth in subsequent chapters.

1.9.1 Psychotherapy

Nelson-Jones (2001) describes psychotherapy broadly as the healing of the mind or the soul. Counselling is defined as assisting others to improve their well-being, alleviate their distress, to resolve crises, increase their abilities to solve problems and make decisions (Brammer, Abrego & Shostrom, 1993). Reber and Reber (2001) add that psychotherapy is an inclusive method of healing mental, emotional and behavioural disorders by using different scientifically evidenced techniques that have palliative and curative effectiveness. In other words counselling and psychotherapy are concerned with promoting the psychological well-being of a client.

Psychotherapy requires exacting and complex skills of practitioners, its application requires the practitioner's ability to offer empathy, understanding and benevolent direction (Novelis, Rojwicz & Peele, 1993). Psychotherapy is the way to treat people with mental disorders by helping them understand their mental distress. It teaches strategies and gives people tools to deal with stress and unhealthy thoughts and behaviours, helping people manage their symptoms better and function more effectively on a daily basis. Psychotherapy is a primarily interpersonal treatment that is based on psychological principles and involves a trained therapist and a client who has a problem, or complaint; it is intended by the therapist to be remedial for the client's problem; and it is adapted or individualized for the particular client (Wampold, 2001).

Given these points, psychotherapy can be summarised as being a long term interpersonal treatment performed by a trained psychotherapist to assist another person to remedy thoughts, emotions or behaviours. In this study I use psychotherapy instead of counselling because the two are similar but counselling refers to a more short term intervention. This study is conducted on practitioners of psychotherapy because it seeks to investigate experiences of psychotherapists in their practice. Since the participants in this study are psychologists in the clinical, counselling and educational categories, all have been trained in and have experience of conducting psychotherapy in their practices.

1.9.2 Therapeutic frame/boundaries

Psychotherapy is embedded within rigid ethical principles because it works with people and there is a history of some clients being harmed in the process that is designed to be healing. It is therefore crucial that there be principles of practice such as ethics. Some principles are rigid and others are more flexible in that they do not lead to harm if they are not followed precisely. These more flexible arrangements are termed therapy frames and are also called ground rules or boundaries. In this study, I focus more on these principles since they are more flexible.

The therapeutic frame relates to the professional and ethical conduct of the psychotherapist and contributions to the safety of the endeavour for both therapist and the client Langs, 1979 (cited in Siegelman, 1990). A sound therapy frame works by providing a healing relationship that is unambiguous, consistent and reliable (Jordan and Marshall, 2010).

1.9.3 Culture and worldview

According to Semenya and Mokwena (2012) culture is a concept that is difficult to define. Mkhize (2003) suggests that culture refers to the ways in which different societies understand their collective systems of meaning and meaning-making, as well as their collective ways of valuing and understanding the world that they inhabit. Leach and Aten (2010, 2) remark on the many definitions that exist, suggesting that “Because the term culture has often been equated with race and ethnicity … we like the term diversity"; and they note a wide range of factors influencing culture, including "sexual orientation, abilities, spiritual and religious issues, gender, and age". In order not to conflate such factors or try to simplify the influences of common realities that lead to variations culturally, I prefer the term worldview, which has been defined as "a set of interrelated beliefs and assumptions" (Utsey, Fischer & Belvet., 2010, 182) about one's existence, relationships with and ideas about others, based upon one's constructs about the world, all formed and informed by life experiences and influences.

1.9.4 amaXhosa

amaXhosa are the predominant group in the Eastern Cape Province of SA. They speak isiXhosa as their language and they are the second biggest ethnic group in SA. Historically, their impact has been most recognised in political influence, tradition and religion in SA through people like Nelson Mandela, Oliver Tambo, Tiyo Soga and Desmond Mpilo Tutu (Buqa, 2015).

1.9.5 African psychology

African psychology is the umbrella concept that is given to the broad terrain of psychology practise conducted by psychologists in Africa (Makhubela, 2016). It is a body of knowledge that is concerned with understanding African life and traditional worldviews (Kazdin, 2000). Furthermore, African psychology is embedded in some principles which integrate religion and spirituality. It promotes a style of living that is about cooperation not competition (Amaeshi & Idemudia, 2015). According to Rowe 2015 (cited in Shajaa & Shajaa, 2015) African psychology aims at establishing knowledge and skills or implementing African-centred psychology, in order to bring about a curriculum that will certify psychologists to address the particular psychological needs of Africans.

1.9.6 uBuntu

This is the philosophy that proposes that "a person is a person through other persons" (translating differently the isiXhosa words in section 1.4). None of us comes into the world fully formed. We would not know how to think, or walk, or speak, or behave as human beings unless we learned it from other human beings. We need other human beings in order to be human (Tutu, 2004, cited in Robinson-Morris, 2019). The very fabric of traditional African life has traditionally centred on community and belonging to a network of people.

Whilst a more individualistic worldview asserts, "I think therefore I am", uBuntu rather proposes "I am because you are, and because you are, therefore I am" (Bandawe, 2005).

Engelbrecht and Kasiram (2012) indicate that uBuntu values include survival, solidarity, compassion, respect and dignity. Survival refers to the capacity to survive in difficulty and hardship through collaboration with others and care, rather than through self-reliance. uBuntu is one of the core values of the amaXhosa that are being studied in this enquiry. uBuntu is a way of life, a universal truth, an expression of human dignity, underpinning an open society (Cilliers, 2008).

1.10 The thesis: A reader's guide

In this introduction section I have outlined the background, the context, the purpose and the methodology to be followed in this study. In Chapter 2, I explore the literature on traditional psychotherapy ethics and therapeutic frames as Western concepts. Ethical principles became an area of concern to me, when I was initially discussing my own experiences of challenges in my therapeutic practice. However, further explorations showed that my central concerns were about the translation of ethical principles into the therapy frame in practice. I feel this is crucial as my study is aimed at challenging those aspects of therapeutic frames that seem to be posing challenges to amaXhosa psychotherapists. uBuntu as a way of living and a core value of Africans, including amaXhosa; and suggestions of how it might be incorporated into psychotherapy are covered in Chapter 3. In Chapter 4, I discuss the methodology that I have followed to explore the lived experiences of psychotherapists in their psychotherapy practise and their use of uBuntu in psychotherapy. I start by giving a brief exploration of Phenomenology, the source of IPA; and then discuss IPA in depth. Thereafter, I discuss the findings of my enquiry in Chapter 5. I have divided this section into six sub-sections, where I start by giving a brief explanation of how I analysed the data. I then discuss the five themes I discovered in my analysis, as my findings. In Chapter 6, I make links with the literature to discuss the findings of my enquiry. Chapter 7 is my final chapter where I weave together my thoughts about the discussion, coming to conclusions and recommendations.

CHAPTER 2

PSYCHOTHERAPY, ETHICS AND THE THERAPY FRAME

2.1 Introduction

In first discussing the scope and topic of this study, it became apparent that the key elements of psychotherapy practice that would be important to consider are those related to practice ethics and to the therapy frame, since these provide the broader framework and guidelines for the psychotherapy endeavour. The ethical guidelines for practice are laid down by the professional regulatory body and contraventions of these could lead to being reported to the HPCSA. Thus in this chapter I aim to acknowledge the existence or identify gaps in the literature on ethical issues, across multiple practice settings customised for the rainbow nation of SA. The therapy frame is also outlined, because there may be some confusion in practice between what is prescribed in ethical codes and what is taught about the 'frame'.

According to the first outline designed for SA psychologists in Steere and Wassenaar (1985), fundamental ethical principles are then translated into guidelines for day to day functioning of psychotherapists; which are expressed in terms of specific regulations for conduct. The therapy frame tends to be somewhat more open to negotiation depending on the therapeutic approach, training and practice setting of the psychologist. It is clear that these two elements could be impacted by approaches to psychotherapy that are more culturally appropriate, hence the expansion of these two topics in the chapter below.

Leach and Welfel (2018) note the lack of literature addressing ethical complexities that are confronted in different settings and with culturally diverse populations. The Ethical Principles of Psychologists Code of Conduct (APA, 2010) affirms that psychologists should practice within their competence; inclusive of awareness and respect for diversity. Here emphasis is placed on the importance for psychotherapists to be aware of the contexts of their clients, recognising that people are socialised to understand themselves as racial, ethnic and cultural beings. Psychotherapists should appropriately assess for the social, political and historical factors that may influence a client, in order of interventions be carefully chosen and applied so that they incorporate culture-specific elements (Speight & Cadaret, 2018).

As indicated in section 1.9.1, Nelson-Jones (2001) describes therapy as the healing of the mind or the soul. Counselling is defined as assisting others to improve their well-being, alleviate their distress, resolve crises, increase people's ability to solve problems and make decisions (Brammer, Abrego & Shostrom, 1993). In other words counselling and therapy are both concerned with the psychological well-being of a client. In SA, psychologists who do counselling and psychotherapy are registered with the HPCSA, and in this study 'psychotherapist' will be used as a term to label such work.

In my quest to make my contribution, I briefly discuss the definition of and the rationale for practice ethics. I then discuss the historical development of ethics in generally followed by the development of psychology and ethical codes in SA. This is followed by the challenges in translating ethical codes into practice. I then proceed to the current psychology-related ethics as specified in SA; which are grouped thematically. Finally I discuss therapy frames, before concluding this chapter. I wish to indicate that this is not an exhaustive review of either of the fields of psychotherapy or ethics, rather this is a selective overview that has been determined by the topic and scope of my thesis.

Since this study is about a section of psychology called psychotherapy it is important to note that psychotherapy is also practised by other professionals such as psychiatrists, occupational therapists, social workers, among others. I will be focusing on the history of psychotherapy practised by psychologists. The following diagram is the graphical overview of this chapter.

Figure 2.1: Synthesis of Chapter Two's design

According to Tweney (2017) one of the founders of Psychology was Wilhelm Wundt who was a German Physiologist and the first person that called himself a psychologist, with the first laboratory of psychology in 1879. The term 'psychology', literally means the science of the soul. This term is divided into two parts: Psyche, which means soul and logos, which means science. In this regard, Doyle (1983) asserts that previously, psychology was a part of metaphysics, and dealt with the nature, origin, and destiny of the soul. Kant (2007) indicated that the object of people's wills rests on the immortality of the soul. From some perspectives human beings may be viewed as spirit beings that live in the body with a soul. Psychology treats the soul, but whatever is in the soul manifests itself in the physical, hence the behaviour which is physical indicates whether healing in the soul has taken place or not.

Other more sceptical theorists (Beall, Blascovich, Loomis, Swinth, Hoyt & Bailenson, 2002, Scheman, 1983, Wong, 1967) perceive the development of psychology as a product of a particularly modern moment at the end of the 18th century, linked with social coercion and the rise of the bourgeois family, which later ascended to become a prime technology of autonomy and self-regulation, without which liberal democracies might not function. Thus when considering the origins of psychology, immediately the reader will be struck by either more esoteric spirit or soul-related descriptions or by more critical instrumental views.

The history of the discipline of psychology indicates that psychology therefore emerged from philosophy and physiology. These two disciplines initiated a tradition of historical consciousness that became embodied in courses developed to teach the history of psychology. The psychologists who wrote certain texts apparently agreed with the view that the gift of professional maturity comes only to the psychologist who knows the history of the science (Fuchs & Viney, 2002).

Marks (2017) indicate that psychotherapy is described in various ways, although it is perceived as an age-old method of healing, the 'care of the soul'. In other words, psychotherapy is a professional process of soul healing; using different methods and techniques that are culturally sensitive. For some, psychotherapy has provided modes of describing personal experience in order to create new ways of conceiving of the self, or of being. Psychotherapy was dominated by three particular paradigms: starting with psychoanalysis; then an alternative movement drawing from behaviourism; and then the 'third force' dominated by humanism (Graham, 2000).

Since the 1980s there has also been a rise in the use of terms such as 'integration' and 'eclecticism'. The term 'psychotherapy' may be perceived to provide shelter for a plurality of practitioners who are more inclined to coexist and sometimes even collaborate, with others who differ in worldview but share the same professional title (Berkman, Brissette, Glass, &

Seeman, 2000). However, the term psychotherapy acts as a gloss, which effectively conceals ontological incongruities and historical conflicts. Speight and Cadaret (2018) argue that psychologists are trained into the worldview of dominant groups bringing this unchallenged worldview into practice. Corey (2005) indicates that most Western counselling theories include an emphasis on individualism as the foundation for maturity, where responsibility rests with the individual rather than the group. This refers to the USA context, in SA psychology is also influenced by its Western counterparts, although these are increasingly being challenged as not representing the perspectives of the majority.

Psychologists should recognize the virtues of deep and empathic sensitivities to cultural diversity and the value of spatial understandings that may be expanded through geographical studies and travel. Unfortunately, too many psychotherapists and students of the subject may have their perspectives limited by relatively narrow national and western cultural perspectives; however, the history of psychology when studied might assist to correct such narrowness in their spatial, cultural, and temporal worlds (Fuchs & Viney, 2002). Rosner (2018) argues that exposure to research and theorising on psychotherapy in Asia, Africa, and other parts of the globe, at least would be a start, to discuss psychotherapy-related issues that span across worldviews. Dominant discourses in psychology are influenced by European and Western thought, which focuses more predominantly on the individual and place less emphasis on the social being (Speight & Cadaret, 2018).

To conclude this brief introduction, it should be noted that: an African worldview would resonate with a definition of the field that integrates ideas of soul and spirit more explicitly (Nwoye, 2015); and this research project hopes to contribute to the relatively limited literature base around psychotherapy, as practised in an African setting.

2.2 Rationale for practice ethics

Reber and Reber (2001) define ethics as a branch of philosophy concerned with that which is deemed acceptable in human behaviour, specifying what is good or bad, right or wrong in human conduct when in pursuit of goals and aims, especially in relation to professionalism. According to Herlihy and Corey (1996) codes of ethics have three common objectives. The first and basic purpose is to educate professionals about proper ethical conduct; practitioners who understand the standards may experience expanded awareness, values clarification and problem-solving capabilities. Secondly, ethical standards promote accountability and practitioners must maintain ethical conduct and encourage such conduct from colleagues as well. Thirdly, codes of ethics assist in improving practice by offering solutions to difficult questions. Allan (2011) asserts that professional ethical codes reveal the professional norms of the profession and are the yardstick to determine what ought to be done by psychologists.

Barnett (2011) indicates that ethical codes are not intended to provide clear and specific guidance or the definitive correct course of action for every situation and dilemma confronting a psychotherapist, but that they should provide guidance and augment values, judgements and decisions by psychotherapists. This point thus illustrates that ethical codes may be somewhat generic and provide the foundations for decision-making in practice.

Coupled with the above, the HPCSA (2016) assert that core ethical values and standards serve as a basis in order to maintain good professional practise. It is acknowledged by the HPCSA (2016) that at times core values and standards may clash and in those cases psychotherapists may resolve those dilemmas through ethical reasoning. Nyawose (2014) suggests that it is important that psychotherapists develop a personal commitment to a lifelong effort to act ethically towards clients. Practitioners are often confronted with ethical principles and standards that are perceived as messy ethical dilemmas, leading to stress in these situations. These require good decision-making skills and often involve acknowledgement of emotions and other non-rational processes that can lead to struggles (Leach & Welfel, 2018). Speight and Cadaret (2018) suggest that psychology needs to change its model of the person seeing people not as self-determined, agentic and stable but instead as shaped by their relationships with others, their values and their judgements about the self in relation to society.

2.3 Historical development of ethics in psychotherapy

Witmer, a founder of Clinical Psychology in the USA around 1896, did work on ethics that led to the development of APA (McReynolds, 1987). According to Dumont and Louw (2001) psychology developed quite spectacularly after the World War II in various countries as an academic discipline, where new specialist areas evolved, increasing student numbers and having more staff appointed. Pettifor and Sawchuk (2006) note that codes of ethics designed specifically for psychologists were only initiated about a half century ago with the publication of a provisional code by the APA (Sinclair, 2003). This development can also be traced in psychology as a profession, in that an increasing emphasis on practical and applied matters became important, including the growth of clinical psychology, in employment patterns of psychologists; and in international bodies, international journals as well as coordination across countries.

Wassenaar (2002) indicates that the first professional ethical code to be implemented was the Hippocratic Oath in medicine, which was in place around 400 BC. According to Beauchamp and Childress (2001), the Hippocratic Oath included ethical elements such as autonomy, beneficence, non-maleficence and respect. Allan (2011) suggests that the professional bodies adopted codes of ethics, which became the major source of information as part of professionalising psychology. The codes of ethics developed in order to regulate what is right and wrong behaviour. At first codes of ethics were spread among practitioners by word of mouth but as the profession developed these codes of ethics were more formalised and then were published.

After World War II, the Nuremberg code was negotiated in 1947, which was put in place to counter the practices where the Nazi doctors experimented with Jews without their consent Leach and Horne (cited in Leach & Welfel, 2018). According to Leach and Horne (cited in Leach & Welfel, 2018) the Nuremberg Code was the direct result of the medical experimentation atrocities of World War II. Research interest in the topic increased because of multiple examples of unethical research in many countries and the proliferation of ethics documents. This was followed by the Declaration of Helsinki in 1964, which introduced the principles of privacy and confidentiality. This was due to problematic and inhumane medical research involving human subjects (Forster, Emanuel, & Grady, 2001).

The Declaration of Human Rights was also adopted in 1948 and these codes and declarations are considered the foundation of good human ethical research (Leach & Horne, cited in Leach & Welfel, 2018).

Wassenaar and Mamotte (2012) state that the Belmont Report, released in 1979 on research ethics, emphasises on three principles: respect for persons, beneficence and justice. The Belmont Report emphasises the ethical principles and guidelines for the protection of human subjects of research. According to Beauchamp (2007) in the early 1980s there were rather four principles that were implemented for broader health care professions. These principles included respect for autonomy, nonmaleficence, beneficence and justice thus there were overlaps with the above-noted report. These principles emphasise independence and to do no harm; to improve the situation of others and to treat them fairly.

The first code of ethics for psychotherapists was published in 1933 in the USA and in 1949 the code of ethics was approved. In 1953 the APA published their first publication of codes of ethics which was adopted by other Psychological professional bodies in other countries (Allan, 2011). The APA code was adopted in Canada in 1986 by the Canadian Psychological Association (Wassenaar, 2002). Britain has experienced similar developments (Wassenaar, 2002). Akhurst and Elwell (2015) suggest that ethics evolved as works in progress that can legitimately vary from culture to culture. Leong and Lyons, 2010 in (Leach & Welfel, 2018) add that ethics codes are developed within cultural contexts and little is known about handling ethical concerns cross-culturally, when specific ethics codes are utilised. This implies that the current ethical codes are generic and are lacking integration of aspect of amaXhosa culture

At this stage, it is important to highlight the functions of these professional codes of ethics. Firstly, these codes of ethics contribute to the professionalising of a group of people and keep the standard and image of the profession. Secondly, they inform the public about what the profession stands for. Thirdly, they regulate the conduct of psychologists and they also educate psychologists. Fourthly, they guide psychologists on their daily professional activities. Fifthly, these codes of ethics also represent a collective authority of psychologists working in a specific area such as SA (HPCSA, 2016). Pettifor and Sawchuk (2006) add that the two major objectives of a professional code of ethics include: to promote optimal behaviour by providing inspirational principles that encourage reflection and decision-making within a moral framework; and to regulate professional behaviour through monitoring and disciplinary action against those who violate prescription and enforceable standards of conduct.

From the paragraph above, it seems that ethical codes are designed for good intentions, mainly to protect humans from being exploited, abused or treated unfairly by other human beings. Having elaborated briefly on the developmental history of the principles and ethics of psychotherapy, in the following section I discuss the development of Psychology and the guiding principles or ethics of psychotherapy in SA.

2.4 The development of psychology and ethical codes in South Africa

Gylseth (2008) notes that in SA psychotherapy was taught in Philosophy departments until 1918, when Stellenbosch University opened the first psychology department. In 1948 the SA Psychological Association (SAPA) was formed, however Black psychologists were not allowed to be members due to the apartheid regime. With such a history one wonders what could be the recurring problems that psychotherapists of African origin encounter, when working with the principles as outlined previously. SAPA played an important role in protecting and promoting the interests of mainly white psychologists in the country and as a result a numbers of psychologists in the country increased (Nyawose, 2014). Wassenaar (2002) notes that the work of SAPA has been credited for contributing to the eventual formal professionalisation of psychology in SA.

O'Meara (1983) indicates that a non-compulsory registration of psychologists with the SA Medical and Dental Council took place from 1955. In 1962 the Psychological Institute of the Republic of SA (PIRSA) was established. For clinical psychologists, a further separate voluntary register was established in 1964, but they were not answerable to any disciplinary authority due to lack of formal registration criteria (Parker, 1986). In SA, Psychology attained a legal status as a profession linked to medical professions in 1974 (Government Gazette, 1974). In 1977 a regulation specific to psychology came about from Act 56, and it was amended from time to time. Since 1992, psychologists have enjoyed autonomy from structural control by medical professionals; however the Professional Board for Psychology is affiliated to the HPCSA. This HPCSA Board stipulates minimum standards of training for psychologists and provides for disciplinary enquiries to be held if complaints against psychologists are received. Act 56 now stipulates which actions by psychologists must lead to disciplinary action and is constructed as a catalogue of potential offenses (Wassenaar, 2002).

The Psychological Society of SA (PsySSA) is a largest voluntary professional body that represents psychology in SA; which was formed in January 1994, out of various existing bodies, thus representing psychology in the newly democratic SA and comprising numerous divisions including clinical, standing committees, branches and affiliates (Gauthier & Lee, 2009). PsySSA's key role is to establish collaboration and collegial links with international psychological associations, at the same time ensuring quality services and encourages ethical standards, whilst building professional relationships in SA (PsySSA, 2011). However, the PsySSA Ethics Committee has no statutory powers; though it may cancel a psychologist's membership of PsySSA it cannot bar a psychologist from practice as compared to other statutory bodies (Wassenaar, 2002).

In the following section I deliberate on the SA core ethical values as stipulated by HPCSA. I also indicate the dilemmas facing psychotherapists that are of African origin about these ethical values.

2.5 Psychology-related ethics in South Africa

According to Beauchamp (2003) four major ethical principles still exist. These principles are respect for autonomy, non-maleficence, beneficence and justice, first outlined by Beauchamp and Childress (1979), and expanded over the next decades in the six editions of their text (Akhurst & Elwell, 2015). Beauchamp (2003) explains that these ethical principles are a work in progress as they evolve; and may legitimately vary from person to person and from one culturally influenced perspective to the next. Akhurst and Elwell (2015) argue that these principles include the many moral norms, aspirations, ideals, attitudes, and sensitivities that spring from cultural traditions, religious traditions, professional practice, institutional codes of ethics, and the like. Vera and Speight (2003) mention mandatory ethics as actions taken to avoid breaking the rules and aspirational ethics as action taken to attain the highest possible standard. In the case of SA, mandatory ethics could be viewed as ethical guidelines from HPCSA and aspirational ethics as located within a well-functioning therapeutic frame.

In the following section I discuss such principles. I draw initially from the first publication of ethics for clinical psychologists in SA by Steere and Wassenaar (1985), who suggested the fundamental ethical principles and the practical principles and regulations for professional conduct.

2.5.1 Fundamental ethical principles

The fundamental ethical principles as initially proposed by Steere and Wassennar (1995) are autonomy, nonmaleficence and beneficence. Kitchener (1984) suggested that justice and fidelity should be added to the list outlined by Steere and Wassenaar. These together are discussed as the fundamental ethical principles. I thereafter discuss practical principles and regulations for professional conduct. In the regulations and principles I incorporate the current HPCSA guidelines.

2.5.1.1 Autonomy

According to Beauchamp (2003) this means the obligation of psychotherapist to respect the decision making capacity of independent persons. In other words psychotherapists must honour the right of clients to self-determination or to make their own informed choices, and to live their lives by their own beliefs, values and preferences (HPCSA, 2016). Steere and Wassenaar (1985) argue that by virtue of their environmental situation or psychological state, certain individuals are deemed incapable of autonomous decision-making. In such cases psychotherapists or other responsible adults may have to assist them towards a position which they are able to exercise autonomous choices. Kitchener (1984) adds that this principle includes more than respect for individuality but mutual respect.

2.5.1.2 Nonmaleficence

Nonmaleficence is one of the golden rules of psychotherapy that means do no harm. This implies that the psychotherapist has an obligation to avoid causing harm (Beauchamp, 2003) and is expected to act in the best interest of the client (HPCSA, 2016). Speight and Cadaret (2018) add that nonmaleficence is directly relevant to ethical practice with Africans. The nature of addressing racial and cultural differences is part of the ethical responsibility of psychologists, where there needs to be sensitivity to the degree of cultural mistrust, which implies that clients can be harmed by what goes unsaid.

2.5.1.3 Beneficence

The psychotherapist must act in the best interest of the client, even in the situations when the best interest of the client contradicts that of the psychotherapist's personal self-interest (HPCSA, 2016). It is the psychotherapist's obligation to fairness in the distribution of benefits and risks (Beauchamp, 2003), benefiting the individual under the care of a psychotherapist (Steere & Wassenaar, 1985). According to Speight and Cadaret (2018) beneficence extends beyond the conventional individual treatment model, to examining the person in relation to their communities as well as the social and political systems in which the psychotherapist and client both exist.

2.5.1.4 Justice

Psychotherapists must treat all clients, whether individuals or groups in an impartial, fair and just manner (HPCSA, 2016). Beauchamp (2003) adds that this refers to the obligation of a practitioner to fairness in the distribution of benefits and risks. Kitchener (cited in Speight and Cadaret 2018 indicate the original question of justice as enquiring about the extent therapists have of ethical obligation to insure equal access to mental health services. This is very pertinent to SA today, with the extremely limited access provided to the majority. Barnett (2011) indicates that this emphasises the need to treat all clients fairly and equally, not selecting some clients for preferential treatment and others for substandard care. The care a client receives from one psychotherapist should be generally consistent with the quality of care received elsewhere.

2.5.1.5 Fidelity and responsibility

This further clarifies professional responsibility. Speight and Cadaret (2018) note that the principle of fidelity is about the truthfulness and loyalty of psychotherapists to their clients. It is also about the nature and the limitations of practice as well as the competence of psychotherapists; and about going beyond what may regarded as a standard obligation of service. It also alludes to ideas of mutuality or solidarity with community. According to Barnett (2011) this refers to the need to act in accordance with the practitioner's obligations to clients, whether they are explicitly articulated in the informed consent agreement or implicitly to include those attitudes and actions clients might reasonably expect from psychotherapist, such as honesty and integrity.

It seems as though the five fundamental ethical principles are concerned with a balance between interests of the professionals and promoting and maintaining the wellbeing of both the individual and the community.

2.5.2 Practical principles and regulations for professional conduct

In this section I am inspired by Steere and Wassenaar (1985) to discuss practical principles that emerge from the principles, influencing regulations for professional conduct. The HPCSA notes that psychotherapists have moral or ethical duties to others and society; which are generally in keeping with the principles of the South African Constitution (Act No. 108 of 1996) as well as the obligations imposed on healthcare practitioners by law. In this section I discuss professional responsibility, social responsibility, informed consent, confidentiality, welfare of the client, respectively.

2.5.2.1 Professional responsibility

According to Steere and Wassenaar (1985) this implies for psychologists the acceptance of responsibilities for the consequences of their actions and to make every effort to ensure that their services are used appropriately. Psychotherapists have various responsibilities towards the governing bodies of the profession, practitioners, employees, researchers, teachers as well as supervisors; highlighting that dilemmas and tensions might result from conflicting demands of these different groups.

2.5.2.2 Social responsibility

Psychotherapists bear a dual responsibility towards the individual clients and the broader society in which they work. As noted in Speight and Caderet (2018) the risk of psychology's greater emphasis on the individual may lead to tensions in relation to the person's relationships and constructions of self in society. Psychotherapists should practice in a professional manner that ensures that individuals and societies are relieved from suffering and their knowledge is broadened in order to benefit them from psychological services (Steere & Wassenaar, 1985).

2.5.2.3 Welfare of the client

According to Steere and Wassenaar (1985) psychotherapists respect the integrity and protect the welfare of the people and groups with whom they work. Psychotherapists clarify the nature and direction of their loyalties and responsibilities and keep all parties informed of their commitments. In order to avoid exploiting the trust, dependency, finances, or sexuality of clients, psychotherapists must remain mindful of their own issues and the potential they have to influence clients. Psychotherapists further avoid dual relationships that could impair their professional judgment or increase the risk of exploitation. As soon as the therapeutic relationship is no longer beneficial to the client, sessions are terminated: this is the responsibility of the psychotherapist. Furthermore, psychotherapists should not discourage clients from seeking opinions from another practitioner (Steere & Wassenaar, 1985).

2.5.2.4 Informed consent

According to Canter, Bennett, Jones and Nagy (1994), informed consent in therapy implies that the person has the capacity to make such a judgment, has been informed of the significant information concerning the procedure, has freely and without unnecessary influence expressed consent and consent has been appropriately documented. Steere and Wassenaar (1985) note that psychotherapists fully inform clients as early as possible in the relationship, of the purpose and nature of an evaluative, treatment, educational, or training procedure. Furthermore, they freely acknowledge that clients have freedom of choice regarding their participation. Moreover, the client gives consent before treatment or participation after the psychotherapist has communicated with the participant appropriately about the procedures. In cases where the client is a minor or for some reason is unable to fully understand the processes, a legal guardian gives consent on behalf of the client and the psychotherapist takes special care to protect such persons' best interests.

2.5.2.5 Confidentiality

This means that the psychotherapist must treat personal or private information as confidential in professional relationships with clients, unless overriding reasons confer a moral or legal duty to disclosure (HPCSA, 2016). Steere and Wassenaar (1985) further explain confidentiality as a primary responsibility of a psychotherapist. They divulge such information to others only with the consent of the client or in cases where not revealing the information would result in danger of the client or others. According to Fuertes, Spokane and Holloway (2013) confidentiality refers to circumstances under which communications between a psychotherapist and a client are protected from disclosure. Corey (2005) describes confidentiality as a crucial feature in developing a trusting relationship between a psychotherapist and a client. Moreover, it is both a legal and an ethical issue although it has its limitations.

2.5.2.6 Competence

Steere and Wassenaar (1985) note that this refers to the responsibility of the psychotherapist to maintain high standards of competence in the interest of the public and profession as a whole. According to Nyawose (2014) the interest of their clients and respect for human dignity place high demands on the competence of psychologists. This is done by recognising the boundaries of their competence and the limitations of their techniques, where they only use techniques for which they are qualified by training and experience (Steere & Wassenaar, 1985).

Psychotherapists should not present themselves as possessing technique they do not have. They also recognise differences among people associated with age, sex, socioeconomic and ethnic backgrounds, thus they obtain training, experience or counsel to assure competent service delivery when necessary. Psychotherapists should also continue to develop their experience after formal training has finished and take reasonable steps to keep up to date with current research and practice by obtaining supervision, attending appropriate courses, and reading current research (Steere & Wassenaar, 1985). Psychotherapists must continually aspire to attain the highest level of knowledge and skills required within their area of practice (HPCSA, 2016). For this purpose, a Continuing Professional Development (CPD) programme has been designed and applied nationally where every psychotherapist is required to accumulate 30 Continuing Education Units (CEUs) per twelve-month period and five of the units must be on ethics, human rights and medical law.

These are the practical principles and regulations for professional conduct, which seem to emphasise how the individual psychotherapist is expected to behave in therapy settings. In the next section I will discuss expansions on these principles, as suggested both by the HPCSA and other texts.

2.5.3 Expanded ethical principles

The following additional principles are obtained from the HPCSA (2016) booklet. Some seem to overlap with the ethical principles suggested by Steere and Wassenaar (1985), but over the past decades these have needed to be further described. These expanded ethical principles include privacy, integrity, tolerance, respect for persons, compassion, human rights, justice, truthfulness, professional competence and self-improvement and fidelity and responsibility, respectively.

2.5.3.1 Privacy

This feature draws from the fundamental principle of autonomy and builds on the earlier guidelines about confidentiality. Privacy is an individual's right to be free from unreasonable intrusion by the government or by individuals into their personal space, information, thoughts, or feelings (O'Donohue & Ferguson, 2003).

2.5.3.2 Integrity

This is a comprehensive term that incorporates professional responsibility. Psychotherapists must include all these values in their practise and character as responsible practitioners (HPCSA, 2016). Barnett (2011) notes that psychotherapists need to be honest and to adhere to all commitments to clients, as well as not to engage in actions that would lead to a violation of the client's trust in the psychotherapist.

2.5.3.3 Tolerance

Psychotherapists must respect the rights of clients and acknowledge that clients may have different ethical beliefs, which may arise from deeply held personal, religious or cultural convictions (HPCSA, 2016). Barnett (2011) refers to tolerance as respect for all individual differences in clients and to act in ways that are sensitive to the implications of these on their approaches.

2.5.3.4 Respect for persons

This item emphasises both the client's autonomy and human rights. This implies that the client must be respected as a human being and the dignity, sense of value and the intrinsic worth of a client must be kept intact (HPCSA, 2016).

2.5.3.5 Compassion

An essential feature of psychotherapy is the need for empathy for clients. Psychologists must also be sensitive to clients regarding their social needs and seek to create mechanisms for providing comfort and support where appropriate and possible (HPCSA, 2016).

2.5.3.6 Human rights

Psychotherapists must respect the constitution of SA as professional practitioners in the country. This means that the psychotherapist must respect that everyone has rights as a human being (HPCSA, 2016). Clearly this is emphasised given the past history of the apartheid in SA.

2.5.3.7 Truthfulness

Psychotherapists must acknowledge that trust is crucial for the therapeutic relationship between the client and the psychotherapist and therefore the truth and truthfulness must be foregrounded in their relationships (HPCSA, 2016).

2.5.3.8 Community

Psychotherapists must endeavour to contribute to the betterment of society in accordance with their professional abilities and standing in the community (HPCSA, 2016). In this regard Vera and Speight (2003) argue that emancipatory approaches would seek to promote mutuality and social obligation. Such approaches also seek to remove oppression and conceptualise problems resulting from interpersonal and social oppression. They further use interventions that change individuals and social systems in order to promote a sense of community and emancipation of all people. They add that the ability to design, implement and evaluate community interventions that promote community empowerment would be a critical element in multicultural competence.

Beauchamp (2011) believes that ethical practices are imbued with moral conviction that inspires the highest confidence, leading to the lowest levels of bias. They are universally valid norms that guide us in making intercultural and crosscultural judgements about moral failures, including morally misguided beliefs or cruelty to others. Ethical guidelines need to be specified in order to make them suitable for the analysis of a context, case, or policy and to fit the unique and everyday contexts of practice. From a SA perspective, it is noteworthy that whereas cultural competences feature in other codes, such as those of the APA, there is very little mention of such issues in the SA guidelines. Perhaps this relates to the inherently multicultural contexts of many sites of practice in SA, or to the fact that psychotherapy was previously only accessible to a politically and economically dominant minority. From either perspective, the lack of explicit reference to cultural sensitivities and adaptations that might be required illustrate that this area needs far more interrogation in the SA context.

It is important as a psychotherapist to be guided by these ethical principles while in practice. However, these principles are mostly general and seemingly inflexible in that they do not consider every case that one comes across. On the other hand there are ground rules or boundaries that have been recommended as the basis for psychotherapies; these are not as rigid as ethical principles. The somewhat more flexible ground rules that apply to psychotherapy are termed the therapy frame.

2.6 Challenges in ethics

"A psychologist shall develop, maintain and encourage high standards of professional competence to ensure that clients are protected from professional practises that fall short of international best practises" (Tomu, 2013, 59). According to Speight and Cadaret, (2018), competent practitioners use culturally specific resources and culturally appropriate knowledge of the cultural practices to meet the needs of their clients. Competence requires responsiveness not just sensitivity and awareness. According to Allan (2011) gaps in ethical codes exist because there is no way that everything that may arise will be anticipated, therefore codes of ethics do not always give answers to every challenge or question a psychotherapist may have. This may be the reason for amaXhosa psychotherapists to experience dilemmas and confusion in certain situations where they are following acceptable dominant attitudes but seem to be contradicting the professional codes of ethics. Rice and Follette (2003) assert that dominant cultural perspectives and lack of cultural competency and sensitivity bring about controversy and ethical dilemmas.

Culturally competent psychotherapists are aware of their own cultures and worldview (Speight & Cadaret, 2018), beliefs, attitudes and skills (Vera & Speight, 2003); and those of their clients, so that they become flexible in their helping roles in order to meet the goals and needs of culturally diverse populations (Speight & Cadaret, 2018). Welfel and Leach (2018) suggest three ethical decision-making components namely: knowledge (which is already emphasised in SA), models of decision-making and the attitudes of mental health professionals: these are not as evident in SA literature.

Since literature shows that psychology was designed for White, middle-class models of human development and behaviour; it has failed to adequately represent the needs of historically marginalised communities (Vera & Speight, 2003). They further argue that there is no rigorous research in SA that has determined psychotherapy to be truly effective for so-called minority groups. In SA, Africans are a majority but there is inadequate research done for modalities that could provide thoroughly relevant to service them.

Challenges of culturally diverse clients are best understood as intrapsychic or interpersonal ones, best treated by individual, group or family psychotherapeutic interventions. These interventions should be cognisant of elements such as issues of oppression, racism, poverty, discrimination and stereotyping effects. A culturally competent psychotherapist attends to and becomes sensitive to issues of bias, discrimination and oppression (Vera & Speight, 2003). .

2.7 Therapy frames

The therapy frame is a term used to describe the boundaries or ground rules that have been developed to provide for effective psychotherapy. Bridges (1999) notes that the psychotherapists' clinical choices and decisions about the understanding and management of boundaries are influenced by the theoretical perspectives they hold. In this regard, Schaverien (2013) asserts that boundaries should be clear to both the client and the psychotherapist. However, it is the therapist who establishes what is on offer, the shape of psychotherapy or what is considered to be within or outside of the boundaries. The psychotherapist's background, formative learning experience, beliefs, fears, personal philosophy and the way she presents herself, all communicate and influence the setting in psychotherapy. However, although psychotherapists in SA may be well informed about the parameters of ethical conduct, they may need to further explore the ethical construction of creative, clinically useful boundaries in therapist-patient dyads. It is in this regard that I find therapy frames to be important to discuss in the context of this study.

In the following section I start by discussing the origin of therapy frames, I then conceptualise therapy frames and discuss the need for these. This is followed by discussing the functions of therapy frames and I finalise this section by describing elements that are recommended, in order to provide effective therapy frames.

2.7.1 Origin of therapy frames

According to Gray (2014), Milner was the first to apply the concept of the frame using the metaphor of an artist's frame. This idea comes from when an artist completes a piece of art, it is usually framed and the choice of frame is important because it performs the function of containing the artistic creation as a boundary. This idea of therapeutic frames or boundaries in counselling and psychotherapy has emerged from practice, with some overlap with ethics.

According to Gabbard (1995) the concept of the frame was developed by psychoanalysts to contain the transference feelings evoked in the therapeutic relationship between the psychotherapist and the client. Barnett (2011) notes that the mental health professions historically held a very rigid and restrictive view of therapy frames in the treatment relationship. In the beginning psychoanalytic and psychodynamic perspectives saturated mental health professions' thinking on therapy frames.

2.7.2 Conceptualising therapy frames

The psychotherapy frame relates to the professional and ethical conduct of the psychotherapist; and contributes to the safety of the engagement in therapy for both therapist and client (Jordan & Marshall, 2010). It is the structure that sets the rules of therapy and circumscribes the participants' behaviours (Luca, 2004) and provides guidance for ambiguous situations (Barnett, 2011). Allan (2011) states that all peoples universally require stable ground rules when entering professional contexts that are unfamiliar, providing a relationship that is unambiguous, consistent, and reliable; which may be considered as a strong foundation of the healing force of psychotherapy (Jordan & Marshall, 2010). Barnett (2011) argues that the way psychotherapists navigate boundaries may have a significant and lasting impact on the psychotherapy process, relationship and outcomes.

2.7.3 The need for therapy frames

Allan (2011) indicates that professional bodies and scholars have produced guidelines that should be followed by psychotherapists about where boundaries should be drawn. These boundaries provide guidelines on who psychotherapists should not treat, who they should not socialise with, and what they should not accept from clients. These boundaries or therapy frames evolve as there are developments in the law and in research findings (Allan, 2011). In order to hold clear boundaries, psychotherapy needed to be conducted in an indoor space (Jordan and Marshall, 2010), where issues such as role, time, place and space, clothing, language, self-disclosure and related matters such as physical contact could all be controlled, normally. These boundaries evolved to articulate acceptable behaviour by psychotherapists, when working in such close proximity with clients, to prevent the exploitation (whether monetarily or sexually) of either party.

There are a multitude of factors that determine whether certain boundaries are appropriate for a particular psychotherapist or not. Such boundaries include the psychotherapist's values, the cultural backgrounds of the various parties, settings and environments they work in. Some therapy frames include a traditional therapy hour; and consider power, mutuality as well as asymmetry (Jordan & Marshall, 2010). Since most psychotherapists in SA work in private practice and may often be consulting with people who have little knowledge of what to expect of psychotherapy, this places the therapist in a position of power. Clients are often not aware of their rights or what the process of psychotherapy entails; therefore practitioners need to take extra care to be explicit about their work and to provide information where they clearly specify the boundaries of the relationship.

These boundaries are sometimes violated or crossed. The former means the psychotherapist may exploit the client by putting the needs of the psychotherapist first and may use the client's vulnerabilities as a means to gratify the psychotherapist's needs; in the process putting the therapeutic process at risk (Allan, 2011). In terms of boundary crossing, the psychotherapist must guard against non-maleficence: in other words, to do no harm and to be able to justify the cause of actions taken (Allan, 2011). Barnett (2011) argues that although crossing a boundary may be perceived as of little concern or irrelevant, to avoid dealing with boundaries for fear of violating those leads to an unhealthy psychotherapy environment.

2.7.4 Functions of therapy frames

Allan (2011) describes the functions of boundaries as follows:

- They provide structure, for clients to differentiate and alleviate confusion they might have about the psychotherapist-client relationships compared to other social relationships.
- They serve to prevent psychotherapists misusing their power by exploiting and manipulating clients to satisfy their own needs.
- They enhance the effectiveness of service delivery to avoid psychotherapists losing touch with objectives of the process and professional judgment.
- They also prevent clients becoming overly dependent on psychotherapists and protect psychotherapists from clients who may experience the symptoms of severe pathological disorders.

2.7.5 Elements of therapy frames

Gray (2014) describes the frame as comprising a private setting, fixed times and duration for sessions, vacation breaks that are clearly stated by the therapist, a set of fee for all sessions and an internal concept on the part of the therapist that what is talked about is confidential within the therapeutic relationship. Examples of unethical dual relationships between client and therapist include: bartering for goods or therapeutic services, borrowing of money, going into a business venture with a client, providing therapy to a friend, employee or relative, engaging in a social relationship with a client, accepting a gift from a client, or becoming sexually involved with a client.

The elements of therapy frames to be expanded upon below are all important, but are arranged according to how events unfold in actual practice in my experience. These elements of therapy frames or boundaries are time, space and place, money and associated matters, language, clothing, physical contact, role, normalising and self-disclosure, gifts and bartering, respectively.

2.7.5.1 Time

Allan (2011) notes that psychotherapists must always be punctual and be good timekeepers and must be consistent in terms of starting and ending of sessions. Policies must be available to address issues pertaining to time in their practise; such as whether they will take telephone calls between sessions with clients; and therapists need to be consistent in implementing such policies. Deviation from these should be due to emergencies or compelled by strong ethical reasons to deviate.

2.7.5.2 Place and space

Langs, 1979 (cited in Siegelman, 1990) indicated that traditionally psychotherapy is conducted in a private sound-proof office in a professional building to ensure total confidentiality, a one to one relationship and absence of physical contact. These aspects are confirmed by Gutheil and Gabbard (1993) as aspects of a conducive environment for psychotherapy. Jordan and Marshall (2010) indicate that in cases where psychotherapy takes place outside the traditional space, these could be viewed as dual relationships. They add that working outside the traditional therapeutic space does not address issues such as power and mutuality within the client and psychotherapist relationship. Jordan and Marshall (2010) therefore do not recommend psychotherapy to take place in natural settings but in traditional psychotherapy rooms, since this assures privacy and confidentiality.

Allan (2011) says that appropriate space between the client and the psychotherapist must be maintained. Clients can be visited in their homes when there are medical reasons to do so, such as when the client is bedridden. A psychotherapist can see a client outside the psychotherapy space when it is treatment-related; for example if the client is acrophobic (having a fear of heights), the psychotherapist can go out of the psychotherapy space to go with the client as part of intervention. Even in this case the psychotherapist must adhere to other boundaries such as confidentiality, informed consent, beneficence as well as non-maleficence.

2.7.5.3 Money and associated matters

Allan (2011) notes that psychotherapists must be consistent in terms of the fees they charge for their services. Psychotherapists must have a guiding policy regarding fees. Their fee policy must be in writing and must be transparent and justifiable.

Should psychotherapists wish to offer free of charge services as their contribution to social responsibility, they can do so provided that it is recorded and is followed consistently. In cases where the psychotherapist wants to reduce the fee for a client, a psychotherapist must be transparent about that and must be able to justify the reasons for such reductions. However, other measures can be taken in the case where the client cannot afford to pay for services, such as spreading the sessions in order that the client attends sessions after the client's pay day. These are all dilemmas for psychotherapists in SA who are mostly in private practice, so need to earn enough to support themselves; however the needs are great, since there are almost no services for the majority.

2.7.5.4 Language

Since there are eleven official languages in SA, language usage and fluency in more than one language can be an advantage. Allan (2011) indicates the importance of appropriate language use in psychotherapy sessions, since the processes of therapy are language based and in order that people feel and are understood. He says that certain disturbed clients may use rude and demeaning language in order to embarrass the psychotherapist, so they can control the psychotherapist. Even so the psychotherapist must use proper and respectful language, striving not to retaliate.

Goode-Cross and Grim (2016) indicate that the use of cultural idioms and a shared vernacular is helpful for both psychotherapists and their clients for effective communication to take place. Madu (2009) explains the predicaments experienced by psychotherapists in Africa. He says it is important for psychologists to practise psychotherapy with Black clients in a way that will address their needs. He adds that healing in the African contexts is practised by traditional healers and diviners and techniques include the use of idioms (language). He suggests that psychotherapists in Africa should be broad minded and maybe even adopt some of those techniques that can be useful in their practise.

2.7.5.5 Clothing

Allan (2011) notes that the type of clothes the psychotherapist wears give a powerful symbolic message. Certain clients may be offended by psychotherapists who wear inappropriate clothes that are revealing or that have slogans on them. Psychotherapists are encouraged to wear conservative clothes when in practise.

2.7.5.6 Physical contact

According to Zur (2007) the major concern about physical contact in psychotherapy sessions has focused on sexually exploitative psychotherapists and the concern that a client may interpret touch as having sexual intent. Touch has been part of most healing traditions throughout human history, but it has been controversial in Western medicine and more so within the field of psychotherapy. Clinically appropriate and ethical touch clearly falls within the standard of care where practitioners who employ touch in psychotherapy must make sure it is theoretically justifiable and clinically appropriate given the client's history, age, gender, sexual orientation, cultural beliefs and presenting problem (Zur, 2007). These psychotherapists must take into consideration the type of setting, the quality of the therapeutic relationship, their own comfort and attitudes towards touch as well as their training and scope of practice. Allan (2011) argues that in cultural environments where interpersonal physical contact is acceptable as a form of communication; in such cases it can be allowed. However, other forms of physical contact are not acceptable where they may be interpreted as intimacy or if they are offensive in some way and psychotherapists are often cautioned against initiating physical contact.

2.7.5.7 Role

Corey (2005) indicates that one of the effective characteristics of psychotherapists is that they are able to maintain healthy boundaries. Allan (2011) adds that it is the responsibility of the psychotherapist to manage boundaries and to ensure that they are not violated or crossed irresponsibly. Crossing boundaries can lead to harm. Moreover psychotherapists must cautiously manage boundaries so that they protect themselves from false complaints, which may lead to them being deregistered from the HPCSA. Drawing from work in USA Goode-Cross and Grim (2016) indicate that psychotherapists often reported that they would go beyond the traditionally defined role of a therapist with Black clients, often serving as mentors and role models for their clients. Allan (2011) suggests that psychotherapists discuss any boundary crossing with their clients and obtain proper informed consent in writing.

2.7.5.8 Normalising and self-disclosure

Reber and Reber (2001) describe normalising as adjusting something so as to bring it into accordance with an acceptable norm. Normalising can play a valuable role in reassuring clients about expected reactions to certain occurrences. Barnett (2011) describes self-disclosure as a process of sharing personal information by a psychotherapist to a client.

Barnett (2011) says that self-disclosure in order to give guidance about the procedure and the logistics of sessions is appropriate. However, self-disclosure also relates to giving further personal details to clients, or disclosing one's own experiences. This needs to be done with due caution, in order to remain the professional relationship, rather than becoming overly familiar. This means that whenever a psychotherapist is self-disclosing, she must be cognisant of the ethical codes from HPCSA. Barnett (2011) adds that there is inadequate guidance provided in terms of the specific actions or information that may be inappropriate in self-disclosure. This inadequacy of guidance may be one of the reasons for dissonance among psychotherapists. Allan (2011) indicates that psychotherapists must be very careful to disclose information about themselves for security reasons; and too much focus on the therapist's material may be detrimental to the therapeutic relationship, thus being a definite boundary crossing.

Barnett (2011) further recommends that self-disclosure must be clinically relevant. It must be provided with caution, looking at the intention of the psychotherapist to self-disclose, how it will impact the client, as well as links to the culture of the client. When self-disclosure is appropriately applied it assists in the client achieving treatment goals (Barnett, 2011). In some cultures not engaging in self-disclosure is perceived as being negative and aloof whereas there are cultures where it is viewed as unprofessional. Therefore the decision of the psychotherapist to divulge personal information to the client should be carefully managed and based on how it will be received by the client. Ultimately it is the client that must be healed from this process of psychotherapy.

In various backgrounds, self-disclosure by a psychotherapist assists in developing the therapeutic alliance and a trusting relationship between the psychotherapist and the client. In such cultures self-disclosure becomes an essential component of multicultural competence (Barnett, 2011). Self-disclosure by African psychotherapists may lead to quicker interconnection with the client.

2.7.5.9 Gifts

Allan (2011) indicates that psychotherapists should discourage clients from giving them gifts and they should be discouraged from giving clients gifts. He adds that supervision should be used as the platform to explore such experience. However stopping clients from giving their psychotherapists gifts may be difficult from the perspective of other cultures, it may be perceived as rude and may be damaging to the professional relationship. In such cases a psychotherapist may consider the context in which the gift is given. It is important for the psychotherapist to decide how to handle such situations before they take place. In the case where the psychotherapist receives a gift from the client, it is important that the client is made aware that the gift will be for the benefit of all the staff members in the office. However, the psychotherapist must consider her theoretical orientation, as it will be improper for some modalities to accept even a small gift from clients; and this sanction should be made clear when contracting with the client.

2.7.5.10 Bartering

According to HPCSA (2015) a psychologist may barter only if it is not professionally contraindicated, or the resulting arrangement is not exploitative given that it may be the client's only mode of remuneration for the psychological service provided. Allan (2011) says in the case where the psychotherapist practises in extremely poverty stricken areas, where clients exchange goods for psychotherapy instead of money for psychotherapy, bartering can be accepted. In such cases a psychotherapist must identify the value of the goods or services the client has used as a payment for psychotherapy

To conclude this section I am inspired by Johnson and Sandhu (2018) who suggest that psychotherapists should be flexible in their approaches to treatment, in that treatment should be adapted to meet each client's needs and capitalise on cultural strengths. Such treatment should include reducing jargon, providing the treatment in language which incorporates cultural, religious or other alternative healing strategies or using a system of cultural values or frameworks to undergird techniques.

2.8 Conclusion

Gergen, Gulerce, Lock and Misra (1996) state that during the introduction of psychology in to developing countries such as in Africa, efforts were made to understand indigenous people's experiences using Western concepts; hence it is now acknowledged that psychological processes are culture-based. Corey (2005) claims that some counsellors have criticised traditional therapeutic practices as irrelevant for people of other cultures. He adds that most techniques are derived from counselling approached developed by and for White, middle-class, western clients. These approaches may not be applicable to clients from different racial, ethnic, and cultural backgrounds.

Maxie, Arnold and Stephenson (2006) add that there is evidence in the (USA) that ethnic and racial minority clients prefer counsellors who are similar to them. Furthermore, some studies have demonstrated that ethnic matching leads to better outcomes (Constantine, 2001, Ponterotto, Kim, Ng & Ahn, 2005), although the results are far from being conclusive. In contrast, Neo and Akhurst (2016) showed that certain clients in the UK preferred consulting with psychotherapists not from their ethnic group because the meanings of issues discussed may be more explicitly clarified and leading to clients feeling that they are able to be more open; and that they will not be judged if they are perceived as challenging their own culturally influenced norms.

Luca (2004) warns that it would be a mistake to assume that modifications in the agreed frame and flexible boundaries for psychotherapy do not have wide ranging implications for practice. It would also be a mistake to assume that an overly rigid framework would protect psychotherapists from behaving detrimentally towards clients. This means the integrity of the psychotherapist is vital for the process to be successful. Berg (2003) argues that in SA different realities and cosmologies are challenges that face many people daily. However, training has been grounded in formulations that are originated from the Western world where emphasis is on individuals, the rational and the scientific and the body mind duality, where the reality of the individual with his or her personal past and intrapsychic conflict is the central point of departure. In their preface to a recent text on applied ethics, Leach and Welfel (2018, xv) note "the dearth of ethics scholarship focused on specific settings and the lack of literature about the intersection between specific settings and culturally diverse populations". My study hopes to add to the limited literature, describing the challenges amaXhosa psychotherapists' face, when delivering services to people of similar backgrounds who are more embedded in collectivist worldviews.

To conclude, it seems as though principles and ethical codes are important to establish, in order for fair treatment of humans by other humans to take place. It seems imperative though to have ethics or principles and therapy frames that will accommodate other ethnic groups, the amaXhosa in this case. In this chapter I have hopefully highlighted some of the Eurocentric principles and ethics of psychotherapy and have highlighted aspects that may need further clarification among therapists of African origin. In the following chapter I discuss the way of living of traditional Africans and how such worldviews might be incorporated into psychotherapy.

CHAPTER 3

UBUNTU AS A CONCEPTUAL FRAMEWORK AND ITS LINKS TO AFRICAN PSYCHOLOGY

" uBuntu is the Soul of African society." (Mnyandu, 1997, 77)

3.1 Introduction

This chapter discusses a framework surrounding the concept uBuntu. This framework is drawn from various theoretical concepts in order to guide this research (Green, 2014). The concept that I draw on addresses common practises among African peoples, particularly in the SA and Eastern Cape Province where the study takes place. I propose this concept should explain a way of living of Africans (amaXhosa), which I hoped would make sense of certain behaviours that are displayed in psychotherapy sessions that are not necessarily acceptable to or accommodated within the traditional psychotherapy rules. uBuntu as a concept seemed to be best suited to the task. This view concurs with Cilliers (2008) who indicates that the concept of uBuntu has become well known all over the world as being typical of African and specifically in SA dominant attitude. Gade (2012) adds that SA is the only country in the world where legal authorities recognise uBuntu as a deep cultural heritage and as a foundation of the constitution.

There is however an argument that views uBuntu as a Philosophical term and as an expression of a lifestyle. This argument makes a distinction between Ubuntu and ubuntu. According to Praeg (2014) the former is a philosophical expression in the postcolonial retrodiction; which is the act of interpreting or making predictions about the past, while the latter refers to living practise or unadulterated forms of African Social life. Letseka (2012) defines uBuntu as a form of human engagement, non-domination and the optimal development of human relations. In this study I am combining the two; that is Ubuntu and ubuntu as I think they are interrelated since the former stems from the latter. As stated in chapter one, I am choosing to use uBuntu as a term that combines the two, so as to give respect to the way of living of African people as well to recognise the Philosophical significance behind ubuntu. I also do not use italics when writing uBuntu because it is a word that is acceptable in SA English usage (Praeg & Magadla, 2014).

In discussing the conceptual framework of uBuntu, there are arguments which I perceive as relevant as illustrated in figure 3.1. uBuntu in a broader framework of psychology could be perceived as part of African psychology, thus African psychology is discussed. Because this study claims that psychotherapy that is embedded with Western principles when applied to African clients seem not to be a perfect fit, I compare African uBuntu and Western ways of living. I thereafter discus uBuntu principles that could be applicable to psychotherapy and follow with limitations of uBuntu. Then the rationale of this study and research questions are argued, after which conclusion is presented as illustrated in the figure below.

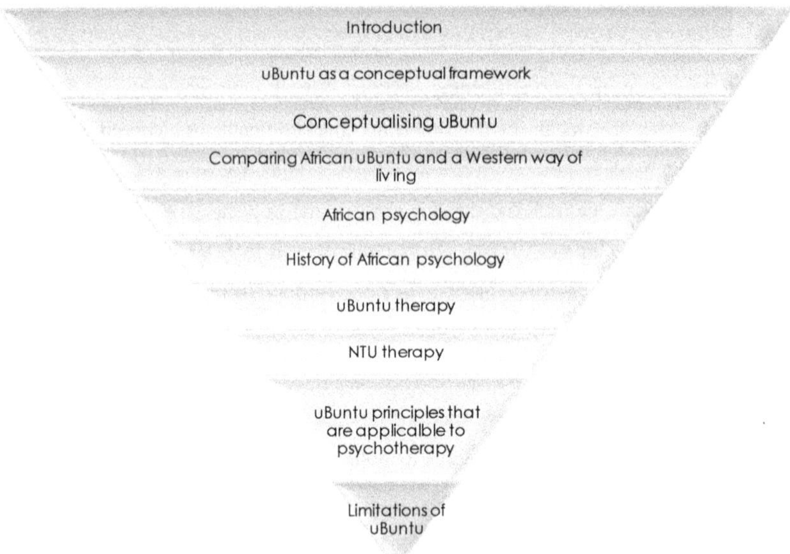

Figure 3.1: Sections discussed in Chapter Three

An increasing number of authors have been writing about the topic of African psychotherapy as well as Western principles e.g. Mkhize, 2003; Baloyi, 2008; Mathebule, 2008; Bojuwoye & Sodi, 2010; Nwoye, 2015; Madu, 2015; Amaeshi & Idemudia, 2015; Ratele, 2017 (to name a few). It is therefore timely to explore current psychotherapists' experiences of tensions between the recommended ways of practice as outlined by the ethical code of the HPCSA (2015), (including ideas of the therapeutic frame), and the expectations and conduct of clients more immersed in practices of uBuntu.

A psychotherapist needs to be innovative and creative to produce a moment of change or an internal shift, which results from a deep engagement with the client. Therefore understanding the culturally influenced behaviours and challenges facing particular clients and the use of frames and/or boundaries that accommodate the client's dominant perspectives may be beneficial to the therapeutic process. Moreover, using African-originated and integrated forms of psychotherapy when working with African clients seem relevant (Madu, 2015). In other words this research has the potential to contribute to the debate around Africanisation in professional psychology.

Neo and Akhurst (2016) note that mental distress occurs across culturally different worldviews and may be influenced by these. In this regard interventions need to be related to cultural values and lifestyles. According to Amaeshi & Idemudia (2015)in a study which was conducted in the USA on minority group clients referring to Blacks, Native American, Asian Americans, and Hispanic people; between 42 and 55% of minority clients return after a single session, compared to a 30% dropout rate for white clients. The reasons for these clients not returning to therapy include lack of bilingual therapists and therapists' stereotypes about ethnic clients. The single most important reason may be that therapists do not provide culturally responsive forms of therapy. They may also be unaware of values and customs due to a culturally dominating attitude that would need to change, in order to help in understanding and treating certain behaviours. Empirically validated, spiritually-oriented integrative psychotherapeutic forms of treatment that include an understanding of the vocabulary, belief systems and the perceptions of clients benefits the therapeutic process (Amaeshi & Idemudia , 2015). In cases similar to SA, uBuntu can be used as a critique of Western modernity (Praeg & Magadla, 2014).

3.2 uBuntu as a conceptual framework

Before I deliberate on this concept I want to justify why I have chosen to use uBuntu (ubuntu + Ubuntu) for this study. I could have used other lenses to view what could work for Africans in psychotherapy; other lenses such as African cosmology or African philosophy, however such are broader frames. Perhaps there would be a view that I should be using the terms African culture because I am talking about Africans. African cosmology is explained as the various ways that Africans organise the universe by means of family values, beliefs, ethos and traditions (Washington, 2010). On the other hand the concept 'African culture' is very complex as there is no single unifying culture in Africa (Cross & Ndofirepi, 2017), whereas the unifying factor that seems to be common among Africans is uBuntu.

3.3 Conceptualising uBuntu

In this section I consider uBuntu as an analytical tool, a way of living of Africans, as well as its usefulness in the context of psychotherapy. I start by discussing the origin of uBuntu then elaborate on the meaning of the concept. I thereafter discus the African philosophy of life called Ubuntu and finalise this section by discussing ubuntu as a way of living of African people.

3.3.1 The origin of uBuntu

In an attempt to trace the origin of uBuntu, Battle (2009) describes the origin of uBuntu praxis by indicating that it comes from a linguistic group of Sub-Saharan languages known as *Bantu* and that both uBuntu and *bantu* have a common root; which is '*ntu*' translated as human and '*ba*' as a prefix denotes the plural form for humanity. The '*ntu*' can also be translated as being or human being. uBuntu , as a Nguni term translates as 'personhood', 'humanness'; which consists of the augment prefix *u*-, the abstract noun prefix *bu*-, and the noun stem -*ntu,* meaning a person (Kwamwangamulu, cited in Olinger, Brits & Olivier, 2007, Praeg & Magadla, 2014). Washington (2010) notes that *ntu* also means the universal life-force or spirit while *ubu* refers to being. Figure 3.2 summarises the segmentation of uBuntu.

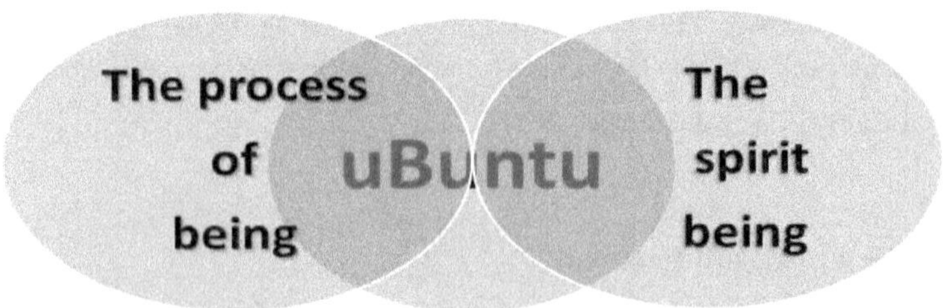

Figure 3.2: Synopsis of uBuntu

In other words, figure 3.2 is trying to unpack that a human being is a spirit being living in a body, which possesses a soul. *Ntu* refers to the spirit being while *ubu* means the process of being (humane). uBuntu could therefore be explained as a process of being a humane spiritual being.

uBuntu may also imply humanity', 'personhood' or 'humanness'. The isiZulu idiom '*umuntu ngumuntu ngabantu'*, or isiXhosa idiom '*umntu ngumntu ngabantu'* (Mbiti, 1991) is translated as 'a person is a person through other persons' defining the core of the philosophy.

Bishop Tutu and utata Nelson Mandela have drawn from in the usage of the term; which is an innate duty to support a fellow human (Carey 2016; Mbiti, 1991; Bundawe, 2005). Battle (2009) and Cilliers (2008) note that uBuntu is also as a way of life, a universal truth, an expression of human dignity, an underpinning of an open society. This means that uBuntu is perceived by Africans as their way of living, the truth about how human dignity is expressed in the way one lives among the society.

Praeg and Magadla (2014) argue that uBuntu is a crucial frame to understand SA dominant attitudes (Nussbaum, 2003) and a wellspring that flows with African ontology and epistemology; which involves humanness, be-ing human; which also gives Africans their special identity (Baloyi, 2008).

uBuntu may be practised in other cultures but the term uBuntu is openly perceived as uniquely African in that is implicitly not expressed as such anywhere else in the world (Buqa, 2015). Table 3.1 below illustrates that although literature notes that the concept uBuntu originated from the Sub-Saharan region of Africa it is a common practise in other parts of the African continent and is termed differently in various languages of Africa.

Table 3.1: Translations of uBuntu in other African languages (Battle, 2009)

Language	**Equivalent of uBuntu**
Shona	Vanhu or hunhu
Duala	Bato
Rwanda	abantu
Mongo	banto
Fang	bot
Bushong	baat
Tio	baaru
Luba	bantu
Herero	abantu
Kongo	bantu
Sotho	Botho
Tswana	Botho
Venda	Vhuthu

This table illustrates that uBuntu is pan-African and is not confined to SA. In this regard, Chikunda (2013) describes uBuntu as involving collective personhood and collective morality, in that none of us comes into the world fully formed. We would not know how to think, or walk, or speak, or behave as human beings unless we learned it from other human beings. We need other human beings in order to be human (Tutu, cited in Gish, 2004).

3.3.2 The meaning of uBuntu

Different scholars (Bundawe, 2005; Lutz, 2009; Gade, 2012) have tried to come up with the definition of uBuntu but resorted in describing aspects of uBuntu praxis. I concur with Lutz (2009) that the uBuntu concept is vague and complex and it may be for that reason that people find it difficult to define. Lefa (2015) argues that uBuntu means that each individual`s humanity is ideally expressed in relationship with others, uBuntu is then to be aware of one`s own being but also of one`s duties towards one`s neighbour.

The following table illustrates further that uBuntu is an African concept and is uniquely used when referring to Africans (Black) people. Table 3.2 is the interpretation of the meaning of how the concept is understood in the African context. To include this table at this stage expands the understanding of the concept and could assist in an attempt to define the concept.

Table 3.2: Synthesis of uBuntu concept (Humanity's Team SA, 2018)

Concept	**Translation**	**Hermeneutics**
Umntu	person	Those who emerged/is birthed from the Great Unknown, from the reed in an ancient marsh or created by God
Bantu	people	The large number of linguistically related peoples of Central, East, and Southern Africa
aBantu	people	In the African sense, when we speak about *aBantu* we do not simply speak of a person in general but rather about a person who understands uBuntu
B		Egyptian element of the soul
UBU	The being	Indicates a process of be-coming as an indispensable part of the lived experience with this becoming and life journey manifesting through the relationship between the person, fellow human beings, their natural environment and the ancestors or God.
'NTU'	African root word	According to ancient African worldview, Umntu (man) is gifted with Divine attributes that are rooted in the feminine principle 'NTU' that points to the causative force, godliness, being-ness, life force, community and essence, and that acts as a sign of *universal resemblance*. As such, man is made in the image and likeliness of God (god + man) which allows *umntu* to be a Divine human being (uBuntu).
uBuntu	Humanity	uBuntu therefore refers to humanity's Higher Self and explains the idea that God is never seen to be outside of the creation and explains the human being's innate longing and yearning to belong. To be human means to be in a perpetual motion of becoming that which one already ultimately is. uBuntu therefore denotes both a state of Being and one of becoming; a process of self-realisation *through* others and the enhancement of the self-realisation of others.

Buntu is rich in meaning as well as how Africans view their humanity. In summary it indicates that a human being is God's creation who has a soul; who is in the process of being, leading to one becoming an ancestor after death; who needs to have a relationship with God, the living and the living-dead and that is done through others.

Gade (2012) perceives the term as uBuntu as a moral quality of a person and as a phenomenon, a philosophy that embraces peace and negotiation because uBuntu favours group solidarity. Broodryk, (2007) and Cilliers (2008) add that in uBuntu self-realisation is achieved through others. Mabogo (in Praeg and Magadla, 2014) notes uBuntu as an ethical behaviour, a politico-ideological practice and a socio-political action; which brings contentment no matter what the others situation may be. In other words, it makes people practising it feel humane and whole.

uBuntu is also seen as the soul of African society (Mnyandu, 1997). Nussbaum (2003) describes uBuntu as your pain is my pain, my wealth is your wealth and your salvation is my salvation. uBuntu is an African Humanism, summarised as humanity or humanness (Cilliers, 2008), ensuring a happy and qualitative human community life in the spirit of family, communality, (Muwanga-Zake, 2009). uBuntu is also summarised by Dandala in the following excerpt:

> uBuntu is a multidimensional concept which represents the core values of African ontologies: respect for any human being, for human dignity and for human life, collective sharedness, obedience, humility, solidarity, caring, hospitality, interdependence, communalism, to list but a few. uBuntu is a statement about being human, about fundamental things that qualify a person to be a person ... Being human is achieved as a person shows characteristics that qualify him or her to be so regarded ... uBuntu is about how you relate to people and is … a fountain from which actions and attitudes flow" (Dandala, in Lessem & Nussbaum, 1996: 70,72).

Bishop Tutu and utata Nelson Mandela referred to uBuntu as the inner core of every person's humanity to move mountains, where Tutu (1999) describes someone that possesses uBuntu as someone that displays generosity, hospitability, friendliness, caring, compassionate and forgiveness. Gylseth (2008) shares Bishop Tutu's definition of uBuntu: uBuntu is everything that is good about a human being. This therefore implies that uBuntu is a soul of African society presented as principles of respect, dignity, collective sharing, obedience, humility, solidarity, hospitality, interdependence, communalism, kindness, and spirituality. These principles are then expected to be shown in people's behaviour towards others.

According to Humanity's Team (2018) the concept of uBuntu is also taken up in 'The golden rule'; "Do as you would be done by" and expresses human relations that are universally desirable. The concept is perceived as the reality of reciprocity that manifests through uBuntu, described as I am because we are, which means 'we are all one'. This insinuates that what is done to one is done to the other. Utata Nelson Mandela describes his perception of uBuntu in the following image:

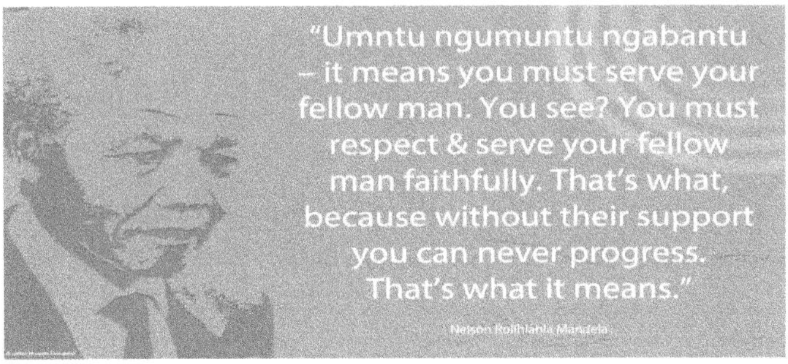

Figure 3.3: uBuntu according to Mandela (Sangweni & Ndlovu-Gatsheni, 2016)

uBuntu as a way of living of Africans, Chikunda (2013) indicates that Nelson Mandela's humanism is a typical example of the qualities of uBuntu. One common feature from the above descriptions of uBuntu is its selfless nature where others are loved, respected, served, and treated as human beings.

3.3.3 uBuntu philosophy

uBuntu in this section is perceived as a philosophy. In other words it is a theory and an attitude that acts as a guiding principle for behaviour of African people. In this regard, Chikunda (2013) views uBuntu as one of the Afrocentric philosophies found in different forms in many societies of Africa and as a key to all African values. Gade (2012) indicates that the concept of uBuntu is essentially an African philosophy of humanism. A human being is not simply human by being born but becomes human through a progressive process of integration into the society, thus formation of humanness comes through the process of socialisation (Dolamo, 2013). Gumbo (2014) adds that uBuntu is passed on from one generation to another, which means the older generation has a responsibility of educating the younger generation about uBuntu principles. Mangena (2016) concurs with the Nicolito and Chikunda and adds that the ethics of uBuntu are consensual and spiritual, in that there has to be an agreement between the spirit world and the world of the living about the operations of the living world.

Dolamo (2013) argues that uBuntu is the central part of African ethics that is steeped in issues such as liberation, development, identity, among others; that has to do with the person's integrity and dignity. In other words uBuntu has to do with the soul of the person that is surrounded by the loving relations of the dead, the living and God. In conclusions, "the African view is holistic in its approach towards the human person" (Dolamo, 2013, 4).

3.3.4 uBuntu as an African way of living

According to Baloyi (2008) Africans have their own way of doing and practising things that is unique, which is informed by their local knowledge, experiences and epistemologies. Battle (1997) notes that Africans need other human beings in order to be human, we need togetherness. For him this means we are made for family, fellowship and community. Likewise, Buqa (2015) illustrates a precise example: In isiXhosa, a person who acts selfishly towards others would be called *akanabuntu lamntu* [that person does not have humanity] meaning that person is heartless, whilst a person who is kind and respectful towards others would be called *unobuntu lamntu* [that person has humanity] meaning that person is 'people-centric'.

In SA uBuntu became conspicuously practised during the Truth and Reconciliation Commission (TRC) which was led by Bishop Tutu, hence he is always mentioned when there are uBuntu discussions. Bishop Tutu used uBuntu as a tool of forgiveness and healing for people who had their loved ones murdered or injured during the apartheid era. Gylseth (2008) notes that Bishop Tutu Christianised uBuntu enlarging it from its traditional conception. Bishop Tutu also came up with the unifying concept in his way of Christianising uBuntu calling SA the 'Rainbow Nation'. In my view this discussion reveals that uBuntu was prominently utilised in SA to heal the nation after apartheid and to unite the destroyers and the destroyed. This means uBuntu also has the potential to be a powerful unifying factor.

African uBuntu is communal, sharing, respect and interdependence are some of the norms. This is illustrated by the ways in which ideas of family are expressed in everyday life. Children grow up with their biological parents, aunts, uncles and cousins. Chikunda (2013) demonstrates this by using the idiom: 'it takes a village to raise a child'; which also means that other parents can execute punishment and unconditional love to children that are not biologically related to them. Moreover, family extends to everyone that shares the paternal and maternal clan name. Sharing is not done with those that are blood relatives only but everyone that is needy. Children leave home when they get married, should they divorce, they are expected to come back home with their children. In rural areas even when children get married they build their house within the yard so they live with the husband's family.

This history of SA has impacted on the styles of living of the people. In my view, uBuntu has been displayed by the SA democratic government by sharing resources of the country with the previously disadvantaged people. I have witnessed the elderly who did not have retirement annuity policies but are at the retirement age, because they worked as domestic workers and garden workers, who earned so little that they lived from 'hand to mouth', being given old age grants. The disabled people are given disability grants. For children who do not live with their biological parents, those foster parents are given foster grants in order to look after those children well. Many of the previously disadvantaged were provided with Reconstruction and Development Plan (RDP) houses and the quality of such houses improved over the years. Moreover, the Department of Social Development supplies people with food parcels so that the poor of SA can at least have food and not go to bed on empty stomachs. This effort by the democratic government continues to slowly return the dignity of some previously disadvantaged SA.

However, uBuntu is not static. Akinyela (2002) states that culture is not a static set of customs, formulas, or traditions. To attempt to locate culturally influenced worldviews in specific customs, traditions and ways of thinking which are not allowed to change, may actually lead to the death of culturally influenced way of living.

As families urbanise since the democratic dispensation, I have perceived some 'un-uBuntu' practises slowly creeping into some elite Black families where they have 'stop nonsense' (high walls separating them from their next door neighbours) around their houses, with alarms or vicious dogs to prevent unannounced visitors from coming in. In addition, heightened levels of crime came with 'freedom', where some Black SA who have less take from the affluent counterparts. It is for this reason that I argue that uBuntu is not static; it has been changing over time. The current uBuntu values therefore seem to be somehow different from uBuntu prior 1994.

Buqa (2015) adds that it would be deceptive to speak of uBuntu and still mistreat others on the basis of their race, culture, creed, gender or status. uBuntu demands respect for human dignity regardless of any outward appearances. uBuntu is contrary to inhuman behaviour; since it is the art of being human. It is probably due to the strong presence of the notion of uBuntu in the hearts and minds of the people of SA that the country did not experience a violent revolution at the end of the apartheid era.

3.4 Comparing African uBuntu and Western ways of living

This refers to the continuum or spectrum of the way of living, as there is no single lifeworld or worldview. In this section when I talk about the Western way of living I refer to UK or USA English speaker's way of living. The above-mentioned traits of uBuntu show that an African society, which is humanistic in nature, is also more community-based and socialist than such a Western society. AWestern way of living is different to that of African in that the dominant features of the Western lifestyle is more individuo-centric. It appears to be selfishness or one looking only after the immediate nuclear family. For example in certain contexts, an extreme attitude was that a baby should sleep alone in a nursery after birth; however, this has shifted more recently due to ideas about bonding. Also, it was a popular view that it is developmentally appropriate for the son or daughter to go and support him or herself by working and living independently after the end of formal education. This too has become more flexible, depending on choices made about further education and economic conditions may also influence the point of expecting a child to become independent of the family. Furthermore, often in the Eurocentric style of living parents are taken to old age homes when they are aging, they sell their houses and may donate the money to charity rather than benefiting family.

Senghor (in Praeg and Magadla 2014) argues that Africans' ways of being and of knowing the world appear to be more emotional and passionate, whereas the Western way of being and knowing the world is more analytical and rational. Moreover the understanding of relationships in the Western and African views differs, in that in Africa collaborations are both vertical and horizontal (Dolamo, 2013). In this regard Mangena (2016) notes that such relationships include an agreement between the spirit world and the world of the living with regard to the establishment and operationalisation of uBuntu in the world of the living. On the other hand, Lutz (2009) argues that although some features of uBuntu are distinctively African, its essential features are not, because it is rooted in human nature, which is common to the entire human race. In other words uBuntu attributes should not only be seen as African values but also human values.

3.5 African psychology

According to Nwoye (2015) African-centred psychology is defined as a vigorous expression of fusing African principles, values and traditions in African reality, traditions and ways of living. In recent years Africans other non-Western therapists have been practicing psychotherapy using Western principles, ethics and styles with their people. For African therapists this could be experienced as a dichotomy, they are born and raised in their specific African culturally influenced worldviews, but trained in dominant Western attitudes, yet have to practice psychotherapy with African people. Contributions of practices related to uBuntu determine how communities live and therefore define their identities.

Mkhize (2003) notes that using only Western principles in psychotherapy when working with African clients may create some tensions and possibly confusions. Nefale and Van Dyk (2003) indicate that dominant Western principles applied to African people might involve unnecessarily labelling certain non-Western clients' experiences as pathological, based on conflicting models of explaining illness, health and healing. In some instances African clients were labelled as pathological due to being treated from a European understanding of health and healing. This may lead to inaccurate judgements about inferiority leading to misinterpretation of the behaviour of Africans (Washington, 2010). For example *Amafufunyana*; which are culturally influenced conditions found among some amaZulu and amaXhosa; suggest that an individual may be possessed by evil spirits, impacting on behaviour, speech and thoughts (Ally & August, 2018). This may be incorrectly diagnosed by the psychotherapist who is not familiar with the African worldview. Since this study is about the use of uBuntu in psychotherapy, it makes sense to explore the history of African Psychology, since psychology may be perceived as a Eurocentric concept and practise.

3.6 History of African psychology

Nwoye (2015) indicates that from the 1940s to 1960s Europeans were dominating in the field of psychology and Africans were uncritically accepting Western approach of psychology. Owusu-Bempah and Howitt (1995) indicate that contemporary psychology in Africa is ethnocentric in its methods, theory and practice and it came to Africa as a complete package instead of originating from the soil in which it is practised. Eurocentric psychology is bound to present challenges when practised among Africans. In the 1970s and 1980s there were a few African scholars that had their views acknowledged in the field. In the 1980s and 1990s it was recognised that not all Eurocentric theories, strategies and principles were relevant in the African context. Manganyi (2016) says between 1969 and 1973, because he was Black he was a qualified clinical psychologist in SA during the apartheid regime, he was not allowed to practice in Tara Hospital; which was a whites-only psychiatry facility. He therefore ended up practising in a neurosurgery ward in Baragwanath Hospital. Manganyi (2016) says these words about African Psychology in SA:

> I know and accept that I am an African and a SA…knowing my identity allows me an ample psychological and emotional room to accept it and reciprocally to accept other people's identities; it is in fact the best insurance against denying identities of others. … Social history of SA psychology and how it became for most of us to see nothing other than super-racists, even among the most talented of the white psychologists of the apartheid era (Manganyi, 2016: 119-120)

Ratele (2017) suggests that there are four orientations that constitute African psychology. Firstly there is more Western-oriented African psychology. Secondly, we find psychological and psychoanalytic African studies. Thirdly, there is a more culturally, spiritually, metaphysically, philosophically inclined African psychology. Fourthly, a more materialist, political, or critical African psychology exists. In other words although African psychology is part of the university curriculum, it is still mostly Western-oriented. A great deal of work needs to be done in order for psychology in Africa to be context relevant, judging from the history of psychology as a discipline.

Arrendondo (1998) notes that even though an increasing number of Black psychologists are being trained, Black people in SA have not been exposed to psychological services as extensively as the white community due to the constraints of the apartheid regime. Given SA's multicultural nature, conducting psychotherapy with clients who ascribe to worldviews that are non-Western in origin will pose challenges. Many South Africans view traditional (Western) counselling modalities as neither culturally sensitive nor empowering to Africans. Nwoye (2015) adds that African psychotherapy must accommodate Africans' understanding of successful living in contemporary Africa.

Since 2000 we have been striving to go beyond African or Eurocentric traditions to develop theories, approaches, strategies and new concepts to confront the current challenges of modern African environment, for the new people of Africa (Nwoye, 2015). This is the attempt to help post-apartheid and contemporary African people to recognise and appreciate the strengths, weaknesses, opportunities, threats and dilemmas of the current African environments (Nwoye, 2015). Carey (2016) states that uBuntu in SA has been used as an antidote to the apartheid system since it served as a core and guiding principle in the Truth and Reconciliation Commission; which helped in healing some deep wounds of apartheid to Black SA. Somni and Sandlana (2014) indicate that such uBuntu principles have been commended on and applied in various contexts worldwide and they play a vital role in dealing with psychosocial problems. Nwoye (2012) mentions that inclusion of African Psychology in universities curriculum might open spaces for enriching and extending scope of the psychology discipline. This inclusion might also put African psychology in a position of moving on from the spell of colonialism.

Given this history of African psychology, I conclude this section with the following quote: "Psychotherapists in Africa should be broad-minded in their definition of psychotherapy to include some effective emotional healing activities of the African traditional healers / rulers, religious faith healers and the in-Africa-originated forms of psychotherapy " Madu (2009:8). With this in mind, I propose an inclusive approach that will treat an African person as a whole that is spirit, body and soul.

In the above sections I have indicated the importance of incorporating uBuntu while working with Africans. uBuntu cannot be separated from Africans; it is part of who they are. This indicates that practising psychotherapy with Africans in SA which excludes uBuntu might not work, even though uBuntu is not static. In this regard, Nefale and Van Dyk (2005) propose uBuntu Therapy; which is discussed in the next section.

3.7 uBuntu therapy

This model perceives a human being holistically and suggests ways uBuntu therapy could be conducted for different types of problems. It also incorporates some African traditional rituals as approaches that could be used in psychotherapy. Africans are community or group oriented and therefore benefit on things that involves groups. In this regard, Wolff (2014) suggests that group counselling interventions are also conducive to collectivist worldviews that are often found in SA culture.

Makhubela (2016) suggests that since it has not yet been able to stand on its own, a strong aspect of African psychology could be uBuntu therapy. Nefale and Van Dyk (2005) note that the uBuntu model of psychotherapy embraces Western theories and techniques and attempts to adapt them to the African clients' unique situation and context, often calling for an integrated approach to psychotherapy.

Makhubela (2016) suggests that psychology be established as a universal science, because it is taught and practised in many countries around the world and therefore its principles should supersede national limits. This means uBuntu could be integrated with the existing principles to come up with a product that will be suitable for other nationalities in Africa.

Buqa (2015) quotes Maluleke, speaking in a colloquium as saying that uBuntu should not be this nice thing that people just say anytime they want, uBuntu should challenge the *status quo*. This insinuates that most psychotherapy approaches that are practised in Africa do not include most of uBuntu principles, that is what should be challenged and rectified. Therapy can be used to assist African families, groups and community members by utilising various techniques to deal with conflicts at psychotheological, intrapsychic and interpersonal levels. Madu (2015) indicates that the aim of using uBuntu therapy is to heal clients on the psychotheological, intrapsychic and interpersonal aspects of life involving culturally relevant, philosophical, religious and psychotherapeutic concepts using uBuntu principles. Moreover, uBuntu therapy was developed for the client who struggles with conflicts between the African traditional worldview and the hybrid, modern worldview, with its influences from the USA and beyond.

Nefale and Van Dyk (2005) suggest a healing instrument that has three useful forms of psychotherapy for treating African people. According to Nefale and Van Dyk (2005) and Van Dyk & Matoane (2014) in uBuntu Therapy a relationship between God or ancestors, called psychotheological becomes crucial. This is followed by an intrapsychic relationship that includes the self-image, confidence level, ego levels which influence the functioning levels of the client. Then there is an interpersonal level where a client deals with issues such as rejection, rigid family or group structure, power struggle among others. In these cases the uBuntu Therapist uses various suggested techniques such as life script, mandala dance, art and systematic approach on family. Mismatch, unfinished business, story-telling, insight, ego empowerment and unfinished business are also some of the theories and techniques used in uBuntu Therapy.

I have chosen to expand on the ideas of uBuntu Therapy because this has been best explained by these authors.

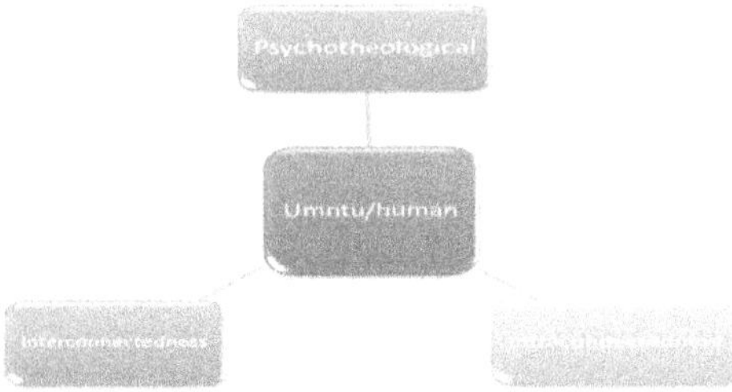

Figure 3.4: Three dimensions of a human being (Nefale &Van Dyk, 2005)

The absence of uBuntu leads to tensions, conflicts, frustrations a disintegrated and disgruntled relationship within the community. The building of good interpersonal relationships lead to a psychological well-being. This affirms the axiom: *Umntu ngumntu ngabantu* meaning no person is an island.

3.8 NTU therapy

As explained in Table 3.2, 'NTU" is an African root word that points to the causative force, godliness, being-ness, life force, community and essence, and acts as a sign of universal resemblance. Utsey, Fischer and Belvet (2010) suggest that the NTU therapy approach is derived from the Afrocentric view of healing; which views an individual as emotional and spiritual bound thus the person cannot be healed without harmony. It also emphasises the interconnectedness between the mind, body and spirit as a holistic model that need to be in harmony. It uses non-mainstream techniques like herbal therapy, meditation, affirmations, visualisation and acupuncture and spiritual reading, if the therapist is skilled in such. Such techniques that blend Eastern philosophies and Western counselling techniques aim to reach balance and harmony both intra-psychically and interpersonally for clients. Thus these approaches have central principles such as harmony, balance, interconnectedness and authenticity, which work towards optimal psychological functioning of harmony, awareness, alignment, actualisation and synthesis.

3.9 uBuntu principles that are applicable to psychotherapy practice

Scholars have previously written about the importance of uBuntu in psychotherapy. In this regard Muzawange-Zake (2009) notes that the uBuntu concept is being used to explore how aspects of African dominating perspectives might be incorporated into psychotherapy, thereby acknowledging the importance of culturally dominant attitudes in self-definition as well as mental health (Gureje & Alem, 2000) and rendering these the necessary respect they deserves.

Thabede, (2008) indicates the following five rationales for modified approaches. Firstly, there is a need to create space for the helping professions in SA and maybe in other parts of the continent that have experienced the subjugation of colonisation, where African culture-based epistemologies have been marginalised to develop ideas such as the African culture-based theories of clinical intervention. Secondly, it is also important to acknowledge the significance of African culture in providing psychosocial services to the African people and to accept that phenomena can be viewed from the point of view of the Africans themselves. Thirdly, Afrocentrism affirms the validity of the African worldview and epistemology as an alternative perspective to understanding phenomena. African epistemologies should thus be utilised in psychotherapy that are based on uBuntu as a core value of Africans. Fourthly, it is necessary to accommodate the Afrocentric perspectives as a significant part of the knowledge base and practice alongside current Eurocentric intervention theories and practices. Fifthly, it is fruitful to predicate the theory and practice of the helping professions in SA on African worldviews, so that the helping professions will better reflect the worldview and culturally influenced values of those who mostly are recipients of mental health services in SA.

The above acknowledges that African cultural knowledge is important in addressing the psychological, intellectual, spiritual and emotional needs of African people. This will move away from foreign frameworks and notions used to analyse Africans' psychological, social and psychosocial problems, in order to develop a multicultural curriculum for the helping professions, with an emphasis on African culturally influenced attitudes (Thabede, 2008). Having discussed what some of the scholars that have written about uBuntu in psychotherapy, I think when practising psychotherapy with an Africans, the psychotherapist might need to be cognisant of certain principles which are some of the proposed principles of uBuntu in psychotherapy such as interconnectedness, respect, spirituality, among others as suggested by authors such as Ramose, (1999), Nussbaum, (2003), Cilliers, (2008), Gade, (2012), Engelbrecht and Kasiram (2012), Praeg (2014) and Buqa, (2015). Somni and Sandlana (2014) indicate that such uBuntu principles have been commended and applied in various contexts worldwide and they play a vital role in dealing with psychosocial problems. These principles influence the way amaXhosa think and feel about their problems and how they resolve or deal with such challenges.

uBuntu praxis is not limited to the principles noted above. There are more practises that fit under an uBuntu umbrella. Kemmis (2010) notes that praxis is a form of conscious, self-aware action, in other words it is a form of practicing ideas. Most African clients can identify with these culturally influenced practices hence psychotherapists who draw practice ideas from uBuntu sometimes find them useful. In uBuntu praxis people find fulfilment in their interaction with other people, the essence is that a culturally competent psychotherapist does not only provide for herself but also enables the community by sharing his or her own good fortune and wealth with others within the community (Engelbrecht & Kasiram, 2012).

3.10 Limitations of uBuntu

Lutz (2009) argues that one of the criticisms of the concept of uBuntu is that it is vague. "The trouble is that uBuntu seems to mean almost anything one chooses." Buqa (2015) notes that the spirit of uBuntu or people-centricity has been challenged by a consumer-centric notion, as most in SA seem to be driven by material possessions. Engelbrecht and Kasiram (2012) note that communities in the urban and township areas are experiencing culture-change practises, as their lives have transformed and some are now seen as more successful. Some Africans due to their financial status seem to take on trends of Western life, which is more individualistic in nature.

Keevy (in Praeg & Magadla, 2014) indicates that uBuntu is deep-seated in a patriarchal worldview where the family grants males authority and power over women. This aspect can prove problematic in a society where gender equality is valued. Keevy (in Praeg & Magadla, 2014) also notes that in uBuntu practising communities, outsiders are not seen as equals or brothers and sisters. This speaks to discrimination against people who do not belong or that do not do what is expected of them in their communities.

> It is through openness to our own life experiences that we are moved to challenge our historically and culturally situated ways of knowing and understanding. When we are able to bring together the horizon of the known with the horizon of the unknown, we are prepared to experience, amongst other things, a shattering of prior ways of knowing and understanding (Holroyd, 2007).

In my view this quote means that even though psychotherapy is an unfamiliar territory for Africans, Africans are willing to experience it and maybe bring it together with the known ways of healing for Africans. African psychotherapists are not seen as outsiders in the uBuntu practising communities even though they bring methods of healing that are foreign.

Ratele (2017) suggests that in SA the struggle is against apartheid psychology where the ultimate goals in searching for an African psychology is to build a relevant, appropriate, socio-politically conscious, transformed, or decolonised discipline and profession.

3.11 Rationale for this study

An increasing number of authors have started writing about the topic of African psychology and Western principles (Mkhize, 2003; Baloyi, 2008; Mathebule, 2008; Nwoye, 2015; Ratele, 2017). Suggestions of how this topic should be taken further have been made. It is timely to explore current psychotherapists' experiences of the tensions between recommended ways of practising psychotherapy (as outlined by the ethical code of the HPCSA, 2015) including therapeutic frame, as in Gray, (2014), and the expectations and conduct of clients more immersed in the practises of uBuntu. A psychotherapist needs to be innovative and creative to produce a moment of change or an internal shift which result from a deep engagement with the client (Gray, 2014). Neo and Akhurst (2016) add that it is important sometimes to adapt modalities to suit the cultural needs of clients. Therefore understanding the traditional world view and use of frames and or boundaries that are accommodative of the client's culturally influenced practices may be beneficial to the therapeutic process.

Madu (2015) notes that there are no training institutions in Africa to train African psychotherapists formal psychotherapy. Pillay (2017) suggest five areas that require an urgent decolonial orientation to introduce new forms of practice such as curriculum, research, selections, interventions, and attitudes. Madu (2015) claims that no proper attention given to adaptation of western psychotherapy forms for use in African-culture-based forms of psychotherapy. He adds that psychotherapeutic activities in Africa are inadequately documented. Publishing books in African psychotherapy have been a challenge due to financial constraints in Africa.

To conclude, African scholars must begin producing theories that reflect African traditions of thought (Ally & August, 2018). Moreover, Ratele (2017) suggests that in light of the call for the decolonisation of higher education in SA, students, teachers, researchers, therapists could design African psychology university courses, research, professional programmes and therapies, as well as networks. This needs to be done as an attempt to explicate what appear to be basic misperceptions about African psychology and to positively build a psychotherapy that will be more relevant to the majority of people in SA.

3.12 Research questions

The following research questions have been designed in order to investigate gaps in the existing literature.

1. What are the original principles and ethics applied to psychotherapy and how do these cause dissonance among psychotherapists that are of African origin?
Through this question I intended to capture the original or Western principles and ethics that are currently used in psychotherapy. I also intend to raise recurring problems that psychotherapists of African origin encounter when working with these principles. This research question also allows the space to discuss how such ethics or principles are causing dissonance to psychotherapists of African origin.

2. What uBuntu principles are applicable to psychotherapy practice experienced by psychotherapists?
This research question strives to adapt to the style of living of amaXhosa as part of the African nation. Due to the fact that the Western principles of psychotherapy addressed by research question 1 do not fully accommodate Africans, research question 2 then is designed

to suggest principles of psychotherapy that could work for amaXhosa psychotherapists in their practice.

3. What are the experiences of psychotherapists (positive and negative) regarding incorporating uBuntu into their practice?
This research question is designed to elucidate the experiences of ama Xhosa psychotherapists when they have used some principles of the style of living of amaXhosa indicated in research question 2.

4. What can the study recommend in relation to incorporating uBuntu into psychotherapy?
This research question is aimed at coming up with suggestions about the principles of psychotherapy that are suitable for Africans, as derived from the experiences of the participants of this study. It is hoped that a psychotherapy model that could work with psychotherapists of African origin will be suggested.

3.13 Conclusion

To draw the aforementioned ideas together, Cilliers (2008) states that although uBuntu originated in the pre-colonial African rural settings it is still a popular notion in view of the restructuring of post-apartheid SA. uBuntu is unique to Africa (Kwamwangamulu, 2007) it determines how communities live and defines the identity of Africans (Mkhize, 2003). Bolden (2014) describes uBuntu in three concepts: interdependence, inclusivity and inter-subjectivity respectively. He describes interdependence as a relational philosophy of constructivist ontology where subjective and emotional appreciation of human experience rather than privileging objectivity and rationality. Inclusivity is an expressive value of collaboration, cooperation and community; which espouses an ethos of care and respect for others and the importance of solidarity in the face of adversity. Inter-subjectivity focuses on the relationship between the individual and the collective, rather than privileging one over the other.

Furthermore, Nussbaum (2003) notes that uBuntu is something important that Africa has, to contribute to the change of heart needed in the world

Finally, I refer to a quote by Malito and Kwindingwi, (2013) because it encapsules my aspirations in doing this research:

During colonialism and the apartheid era, Black people and their values were greatly undermined. The discourse on uBuntu was therefore aimed at restoring human dignity and the values of humanness. uBuntu was seen as an antithesis of apartheid and the degrading statutes of colonialism. uBuntu was employed to show that colonialism and the apartheid system was dehumanising and therefore needed to be abandoned. The post-apartheid SA has adopted this uBuntu discourse as the foundation for transformation in all spheres of life. Since 1994 there has been a drive towards the revival of values that were lost or demeaned during colonialism and apartheid. There has been a renewed interest and appreciation of African worldview, identity and values. As a result of this quest, description and affirmation of uBuntu as an African ethic has received a lot of attention and prominence.

CHAPTER 4

METHODOLOGY

4.1 Introduction

In this chapter I discuss how I worked with my participants to generate data in order to respond to my research topic, namely the experiences of psychotherapists regarding uBuntu in their psychotherapy practice. I further discuss how I analysed the data. Creswell (2003) suggests that in doing research the researcher answers questions such as: what knowledge claims are made by the researcher, what strategies of inquiry will inform the procedures of doing research and what methods of data collection and analysis are followed in doing research?

I start by discussing phenomenology as a research methodology and situate it in the qualitative research paradigm. I go on to discuss Interpretative Phenomenological Analysis (IPA) in detail as the analytical lens for the study. I further discuss methods that I used to generate data. Moreover, I discuss data collection, as well as ethical considerations. Figure 4.1 below illustrates how this chapter is designed:

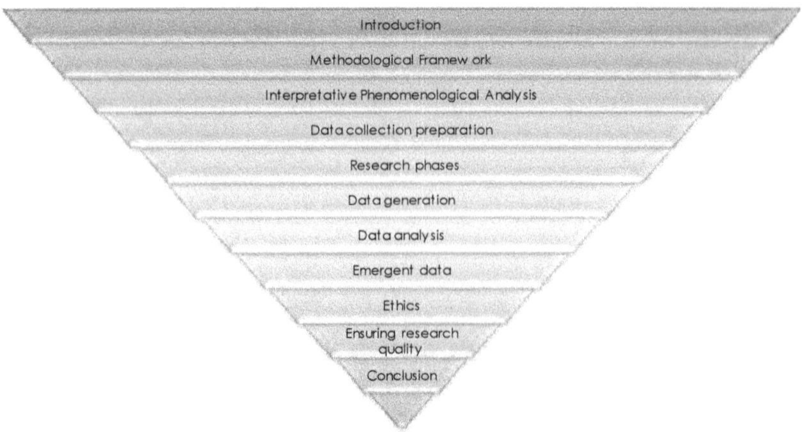

Figure 4.1: The design of the methodology chapter

4.2 Methodological framework

4.2.1 Phenomenology as a research method

In this section I discuss the research paradigm where I start by giving a brief description of phenomenology as a research method and place it within the qualitative model. Figure 4.2 illustrates that the study is located in qualitative research, so I provide a deeper description of phenomenology; thereafter a detailed account of Interpretative Phenomenological Analysis is given.

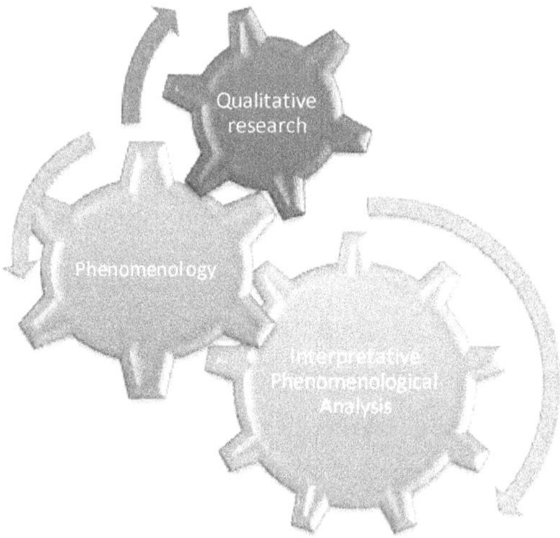

Figure 4.2: Methodological framework design

A wide variety of qualitative research methodologies exist. This study takes the route of phenomenology as it seeks to explore psychotherapists' experiences and their meaning-making Thompson, Locander & Pollio, 2010, (cited in Chang, & Horng, 2010).) about the use of uBuntu principles in psychotherapy. Phenomenology is a rich and complex philosophy, which has been taken up by psychology and other social sciences and has been developed as an approach as well as research method. Creswell (2014) describes phenomenological research as a design of inquiry that emanated from philosophy and psychology, which synthesises the essence of the experiences for several individuals who have all experienced the phenomenon in question. In other words, phenomenology is the philosophical study of being, of existence and experience (Larkin & Thompson, 2012).

Phenomenology was introduced by Lambert in the eighteenth century as a science of appearances (Hsu, 2008). Husserl, in the early twentieth century developed it, as an eidetic method that looks into different parts of the phenomena (Wertz, et. al, 2011). This provides for vivid accounts of memories and images by participants. Lawthom and Tindall (2011) add that it is through our experiencing of our world that we come to know it. Existential phenomenology, which Heidegger (the follower of Husserl) was concerned about, included existential philosophy and hermeneutics (Pietkiewicz & Smith, 2012). According to Pringle, Drummond, McLafferty and Hendry (2011) phenomenology uncovers meanings and the interpretation of the meaning is called hermeneutics. Heidegger's emphasis was on the individual's existence, freedom and choice to make sense of the meanings of existential issues, and thus to try to make rational decisions despite existing in an irrational universe. One needs to comprehend the mind-set of a person through language, by which one deliberates about one's experiences of the world in order to translate his or her message (Kennewick, Kennewick & Freeman, 2008).

Pietkiewicz and Smith (2012) suggest that Heidegger explored the concept of freedom, which specified that humans are embedded in their worlds to such an extent that subjective experiences are indistinguishably linked with social, culturally influenced worldviews, and political contexts. This situated freedom is an existential phenomenological concept that means that individuals are free to make choices, but such freedom is not absolute; it is circumscribed by the specific conditions of their daily lives (Leonard, 1999). In other words, an individual's stock of knowledge is the individual's interpretation of the surrounding social world and an individual's recipe for action is in response to that interpretation (Bloor & Wood, 2006).

Phenomenology is concerned with subjective reports (Brocki & Wearden, 2006) of lived experiences; the richness and texture of experience, which is understood through rich engagement with another person's 'lifeworld' (Lawthom & Tindall, 2011). This means the immediate experiences, activities, and contacts that make up the world of an individual or corporate life or the world of concrete experience as lived by people. Merleau-Ponty indicates that we experience our lives as embodied beings making meaning through our bodies and our senses (King & Horrocks, 2010). Phenomenology is interested in the consciousness of the person experiencing a phenomenon or what appears in the cognisant mind of someone engaging with the world around (Willig, 2009 cited in Shinebourne, 2011). There are links between the phenomenon and the consciousness or awareness of the experience by the person experiencing it, which is termed intentionality (Husserl, 1927, cited in Finlay, 2009). Given these points, the fundamental aim of phenomenology is to condense individual experiences of a phenomenon and people's meaning-making resulting in a description of what the persons experienced and how they experienced it (Creswell, 2007).

The phenomenological method involves the state of evoking an 'epoche' which requires the absence of presuppositions and assumptions, judgements and interpretations to allow people to be fully aware of what is actually before them (Willig, 2009 cited in Shinebourne, 2011). The phenomenological method also involves phenomenological reduction and imaginative variation. Phenomenological reduction strives to describe the phenomenon that presents itself in its totality including shape, size, colour, texture and experiential features such as the thoughts and feelings that are in consciousness while attending to the phenomenon (Smith, Flowers & Larkin, 2009). On the other hand, imaginative variation involves an attempt to access the structural components of the phenomena; its aim is to identify the conditions associated with the phenomenon, in other words, how the experience is made possible. This involves time, space as well as social relationships. Husserl indicates that experience should be examined in the way that it occurs; or to put it differently, the essence of the experience is crucial (King & Horrocks, 2010).

All things considered,

> Phenomenology is interested in elucidating both that which appears and the manner in which it appears. It studies the subjects' perspectives of their world; attempts to describe in detail the content and structure of the subjects' consciousness, to grasp the qualitative diversity of their experiences and to explicate their essential meanings. (Kvale, 1996, 53)

Interpretative Phenomenological Analysis (IPA) comes from phenomenological philosophy. In psychology it provides rich accounts of lived experiences about a particular phenomenon (Smith, et al., 2009). This study uses IPA as the basis for enquiry because it seeks to report in detail perceived experiences (Shaw in Forrester, 2010) as well as to understand the structures supporting the experiences of practising psychotherapists. Humans are not passive objective perceivers of reality but they give their own meaning of their experiences in a way that makes sense to them (Brocki & Wearden, 2006).

4.3 Interpretative Phenomenological Analysis (IPA)

> "IPA is a qualitative research approach committed to the examination of how people make sense of their major life experiences." (Smith, Flowers & Larkin, 2009, p.1)

In this section I will be conceptualising IPA, give a brief history of IPA, talk about distinguishing features of IPA and explain how IPA is relevant to my study. Diagram 4.3 summarises this section:

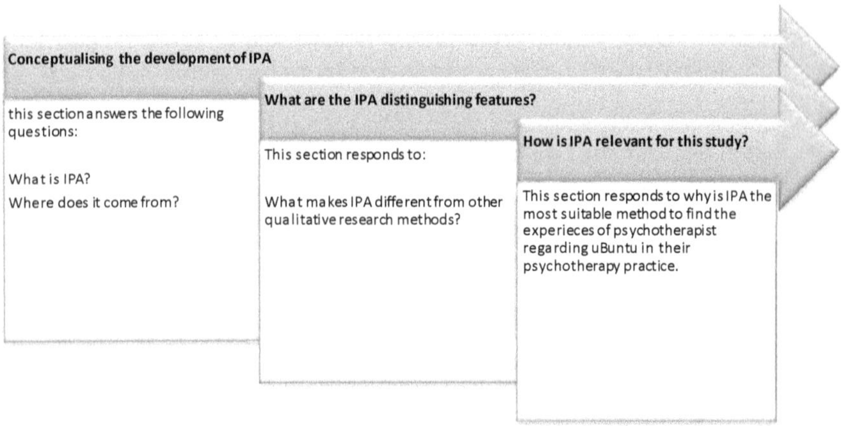

Figure 4.3: Summary of IPA section

4.3.1 Conceptualising the development of IPA

IPA was first used as a distinctive research method in psychology in the mid-1990s when Smith made use of theoretical views from phenomenology and hermeneutics in engagement with subjective experience and personal accounts (Shinebourne, 2011; Biggerstaff & Thompson, 2008). IPA is interested in hermeneutics or interpretations; introduced by Heidegger as well as Merleau-Ponty (Larkin & Thompson, 2012). IPA's central objective is to comprehend what personal and social experiences mean to those people who experience them (Shaw, in Forrester 2010). IPA aims to probe the person's thoughts and beliefs regarding what needs to be uncovered. Furthermore, IPA is concerned with understanding a person's relatedness to the world and the things in the world that matter to the person (Larkin & Thompson, 2009). Equally important, IPA does not test hypotheses and it avoids prior assumptions (Reid, Flowers & Larkin, 2005).

The researcher in IPA plays an active role by getting close to the participants' personal worlds, although it is a complex process (Smith, 2003), by utilising listening and probing skills that encourage in-depth descriptions of lived experiences (Kvale & Brinkmann, 2009).

4.3.2 IPA's distinguishing factors

IPA has distinguishing features that make it different from other qualitative research methods such as its idiographic nature; which is the uniqueness of the individual cases that are being studied and analysed (Shaw in Forrester 2010). Unique and whole accounts of participants are analysed to show their distinctiveness, in order to give a complete and in-depth picture (Pringle, Drummond, McLafferty & Henry, 2011).

A further feature is the way that the field of hermeneutics has influenced IPA. The term 'hermeneutics' is generally translated as 'interpret' or 'understand' (Crotty, 1998 cited in McNamara, 2005). This draws out the concerns and cares of participants, including their orientation toward the world, drawing from understandings about the phenomenon in question (Larkin, Watts & Clifton, 2006). This means IPA is concerned with understanding and interpreting of the phenomenon that is investigated using the lenses of participants.

Once these accounts have been gathered, a double hermeneutic process is followed for analysis, which is a two-fold sense-making process where the researcher interprets the sense-making of the participants (Smith, 2003). The social construction of scientific facts draws from critical psychology and emphasises subjectivities in psychology (Akhurst & Elwell, 2015). Double hermeneutics is a dual interpretative process (Shaw in Forrester, 2010), where the participant gives his or her meaning of the phenomenon and the researcher also interprets the connotations or the gist of the same phenomenon. Coupled with this is 'bracketing', a method used by some researchers to strive to allay the potential damaging effects of unacknowledged preconceptions related to the research and thereby to increase the rigour of the project (Tufford & Newman, 2010). Thus through this, the researcher strives to minimise the influences of subjective reactions to material; carefully working to set these aside through reflection and on-going monitoring of responses.

Bracketing is a method to protect the researcher from the snowballing effects of examining what may be emotionally challenging material. While bracketing can mitigate adverse effects of the research endeavour, importantly it also facilitates the researcher reaching deeper levels of reflection across all stages of the research (Tufford & Newman, 2010), always being aware of the interpretative and collaborative nature of IPA in conducting interviews and analysis of data (Reid, Flowers and Larkin, 2005).

"Intersubjectivity refers to the shared, overlapping and relational nature of our engagement in the world" (Smith, Flowers & Larkin, 2009, 17). Reflexivity is described as the ability to reflect on and consider intersubjective dynamics between the researcher and data (Biggerstaff & Thompson, 2008). The hermeneutic circle is concerned with the dynamic relationship between the part and the whole, at a series of levels. This means that to understand any given part, one looks to the whole; to understand the whole, one looks to the parts (Smith, Flowers & Larkin, 2009). According to Lawthom & Tindall (2011) the iterative process and inductive procedures assist the researcher to develop a perspective of the insider on the topic. IPA is thus a bottom-up, inductive approach that is data-driven as opposed to being theory driven (Forrester, 2010).

IPA is about how people perceive or talk about the phenomenon they are experiencing (Pietkiewicz & Smith, 2012). All things considered, IPA is a critical realist method, which means that it accepts that reality and events exist and people experience those, however the way to access these is not direct (Shaw in Forrester, 2010). In other words certain lenses are used to access those realities, events and experiences. IPA's interpretative stance contextualizes these claims within their cultural and physical environments, and then attempts to make sense of the mutually constitutive relationship between 'person' and 'world' from within a psychological framework asking questions such as, what does this mean for this person, in this context (Smith, Flowers & Larkin, 2009). The overall outcome for the researcher should be a renewed insight into the 'phenomenon at hand' informed by the participant's own relatedness to, and engagement with, that phenomenon (Larkin, Watts & Clifton, 2006).

These components of IPA as applied in this enquiry attest to the integrity and authenticity of this study, providing lenses of analysing data that will be discussed later on in this chapter.

4.3.3 Relevance of IPA to this study

In this part I argue why I think IPA is the most suitable method for this enquiry. First of all, this enquiry is conducted in the field of psychology and it seeks to find the lived experiences of psychotherapists. In this regard, Smith (2003) and Lawthom and Tindall, (2011) concur by indicating that IPA is designed particularly within psychology to account for participants' perceptions of their lived experiences. Thus, personal accounts of participants were interrogated and interpreted.

Secondly, this study exists as a result of my own dissonances in my practice as a practising psychotherapist. IPA researchers are influenced by their biographical backgrounds and previous knowledge of extant literature and thus interpret data through their own lenses when developing themes (Callary, Rathwell & Young, 2015).

Thirdly, I did an in-depth analysis of transcripts taking one script at a time, before proceeding to the next. In this instance, Smith (2003) calls this process idiographic as it entails a detailed analysis of one case before moving onto the next.

Fourthly, I started by analysing the data before I read more broadly about the research topic because I did not want to be influenced by theory in the process of analysis. Smith (2003) argues that IPA is a data-driven inductive approach, meaning research questions are broadly constructed to allow for unanticipated themes to emerge as one analyses the data.

Finally, I aim to make use of the data in order recognise the original principles and ethics of psychotherapy that cause dissonance among psychotherapists that are of African origin. This is to identify uBuntu principles are applicable to the psychotherapy practice experienced by psychotherapists, to also find the experiences of psychotherapists (positive and negative) regarding incorporating uBuntu into their practice; in order to finally make recommendations as to how to incorporate uBuntu into psychotherapy.

This section has hopefully shown that IPA is an appropriate method of enquiry for this study. I now proceed to discuss how the preparations of collecting data were done.

4.4 Data collection preparation

This section is designed to respond to the following questions, as illustrated in Figure 4.4.

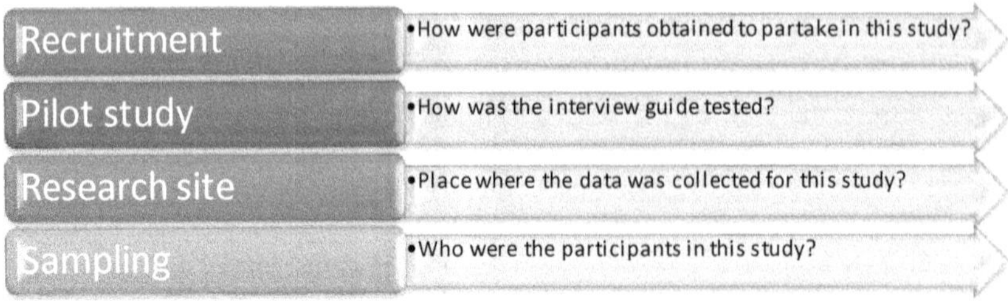

Figure 4.4: Summary of data collection preparation

4.4.1 Recruitment

Participants in this study are recruited because of their expertise in the phenomenon that is being studied (Reid, Flowers & Larkin, 2005), in this case their experience of practising uBuntu in psychotherapy. Smith, Flowers and Larkin (2009) describe rich data as the in-depth information that is obtained from participants when they tell their stories, speak freely and reflectively, and develop their ideas and express their concerns at length. These experiences need to probe the participants' personal as well as social worlds (Harper & Thompson, 2012). Hence experience in terms of years of practise of each participant was considered in this study. I carefully chose participants that had been practising psychotherapy for at least five years, who were registered with the Health Professions Council of South Africa (HPCSA), were isiXhosa speakers and working with amaXhosa as clients.

4.4.2 Pilot study

Before I entered the field I did a pilot interview with my supervisor. This was inspired by the Smith, Flowers and Larkin (2009) advice that doing a pilot study may help one familiarise herself with the interview schedule and to assist with 'bracketing'. In addition Bell and Waters (2014) point out that all data-gathering instruments should be piloted in order to assess how long it takes the participant to complete them. Furthermore, piloting assists to check the clarity of instructions as well as questions and to enable the researcher to remove or rectify any questions that need to be eliminated or corrected.

In this case, we realised that the original interview schedule was quite lengthy and questions needed to be reduced, so that interviews would be rich but completed within about an hour (Smith, Flowers and Larkin, 2009). The proposed interview schedule (See Appendix E) was emailed to participants a month before the interview to ensure that participants were informed of expectations and what the interview is about in good time (Smith, Flowers and Larkin, 2009).This was done in order to prepare participants psychologically and emotionally to share their in-depth experiences.

4.4.3 Research sites

Smith, Flowers and Larkin (2009) suggest that participants be recruited from different locations to increase the diversity of experiences. This follows the principle of maximum variation sampling (Vitcu, Lungu, Vitcu & Marcu, 2007). My intention was to recruit two participants from each of the Eastern Cape towns/cities where there are universities; Makhanda, Alice, East London and Port Elizabeth. As already indicated, these different Eastern Cape cities have people of amaXhosa origin, who are practising among predominantly isiXhosa speaking clients. These cities vary in size and degree of urbanisation, but all have universities where psychology is studied and where some of the lecturers will also be practising and will have experience of the topic. However, my plan to recruit two participants from each of the cities listed above did not succeed as originally planned.

4.4.4 Sampling

In this regard, Willig, 2009 (cited in Shinebourne, 2011) states that in IPA purposive sampling is relevant whereby participants are selected according to criteria of relevance to the research question. I recruited participants who were experienced and who could offer me perspectives on my focus. Samples in IPA are usually reasonably homogeneous; participants tend to have experiential understanding. Reid, Flowers and Larkin (2005) prescribe that participants be experts in the topic being studied who can give the researcher an understanding of their thoughts, commitments and feelings through telling their own stories in their own words. In this case, I carefully selected participants who had extensive experience in practising psychotherapy. Purposive sampling was used in this study because this topic should be something that matters to participants.

Strewig and Stead (2001) indicate that after obtaining information from participants, one may ask them who may be able to provide information, and then they might suggest others that a researcher can contact. I am not very familiar with many psychotherapists who fit the description of my sample in the Eastern Cape, thus some willing participants recommending names of other psychotherapists who might be keen to participate in this study. This then leads to snowball sampling (Creswell, 2007). Henning, Van Riensberg and Smith (2013) affirm that purposive sampling may be adjusted to accommodate snowball sampling.

Pietkiewicz and Smith (2014) states that there is no rule in IPA regarding the number of participants that should be included. The number depends on the depth of analysis of each single case study, the richness of individual cases as well as how the researcher wants to compare or contrast single cases. Smith (2003) states that small samples are more practical for the idiographic mode of inquiry of an IPA study, because a detailed case by case analysis of transcripts individually is time consuming. Because this is an exploratory study, in-depth work with fewer participants was inevitable. Smith, Flowers and Larkin (2009) suggest eight participants at PhD level, thus I recruited eight psychotherapists who are males and females with five or more years of experience in their practice, who are registered with the HPCSA. Maximum variation sampling also guided my decisions as participants came from three different categories of psychology, as illustrated in figure 4.5. Creswell (2007) indicates that in such sampling across diverse variations, important common patterns are then documented. Diagram 4.5 illustrates the categories of registration of my participants along with their genders.

Figure 4.5: Sample summary

4.5 Research phases

4.5.1 Entering the field

I started by identifying those isiXhosa speaking psychologists that I knew; and I also asked for names from other people. I called those psychologists, introduced myself and the work that I was doing, and informally asked them if they would be participants in my study. Those that agreed were emailed the consent form (see Appendix C), the "tape recordings for research purposes" permission and release form (see Appendix D), and the interview schedule (see Appendix E) in order to prepare themselves for the interview. I then called them again to schedule time and place for the interview.

Since I needed to travel to different sites, it became a challenge to find willing participants and to secure time slots that suited both myself and a participant, and to spend at least an hour or more for an interview. Most participants that were willing and available were from Port Elizabeth, East London and King Williamstown (each of these cities being at least an hour or more from Makhanda, where I am located). In King Williamstown there is no university, but being next to the provincial capital there are various government departments where psychologists are employed and conduct psychotherapy sessions. One psychotherapist from another town that was willing to be interviewed did not qualify for this study because she was not registered with HPCSA, although she was experienced in the field due to working in academia.

According to Harper and Thompson (2012) phenomenologists start with the subjective experience of research participants, but also go beyond the text to interpret experience so it becomes more meaningful. The process of interpretation locates a participant's account in a broader social, cultural and theoretical context. IPA studies illustrate rich and comprehensive interpretation, being more concerned with how things appear and letting things speak for themselves. The hermeneutic perspective has interpretations of meaning at the centre.

4.5.2 Data generation

In this section I discuss the methods I used to collected data for my study.

Figure 4.6: Summary of data collecting process

4.5.3 Interviews

I used interviews as a tool to collect data due to their adaptability. One on one interviews were conducted to generate quality information. Reid, Flowers and Larkin (2005) suggest that one-to-one interviews are easily managed, they allow rapport to be developed, allow clients to think, speak and be heard. I designed an interview guide (see Appendix E) which entailed in-depth, semi-structured, open-ended questions. The questions in the interview guide were informed by my bracketed experiences. Berg (2001) suggests that the ordering of questions, language and the general way the interview guide is designed depends on certain characteristics of participants including their culture, level of education, age and social levels. In this case I was interviewing professionals, qualified at advanced postgraduate level, about their experiences in psychotherapy.

Although I perceived interviews as the best tool to collect data for this study, I am aware that they are not without faults. Creswell (2014) points out that interviews provide indirect information that may be filtered through the views of interviewees. Coupled with that, the researcher's presence may bias responses and not all people are equally articulate and perceptive.

When meeting my participants, I used my acquired interpersonal skills used when I am meeting a psychotherapy client for the first time. I tried to create space of positive rapport, where I wanted to be certain that we were both comfortable before we started the interview. This made us relax a bit and get to know each other better, off the record as a means of establishing this positive rapport (Reid, Flowers & Larkin, 2005).

Semi-structured, one on one interviews are conducted in an environment that the interviewee was familiar with, in other words in a natural setting (Pietkiewicz & Smith, 2012), with as minimal interruptions as possible (Smith & Osborn, 2007). My interviews were mostly conducted in my participants' offices because that is the space that the participants chose. Moreover, participants' offices also happened to be where they were conducting their psychotherapy sessions. However one interview was conducted in a hired room, because my participant shared an office space at work and felt that there could be distractions in her office, at the time.

I asked participants to speak as though they were speaking to a friend, to use everyday language and to avoid psychology jargon as much as possible, at the beginning of the interviews. Finlay (2009) suggests that participants' explanations should be first-person accounts, avoiding abstract intellectual generalisations. I also asked participants to select and use pseudonyms, which were used throughout the interviews to protect their identities.

In order to 'follow' participants' ideas I did not rigidly adhere to the interview schedule as the participants would sometimes respond to questions that I had not yet asked. I would then not repeat the question answered whilst still making sure that all questions were asked. IPA allows that initial questions be modified in the light of participants responses, where the interviewer is allowed to enquire about any other interesting areas that may arise. This allowed me to probe more on the relevant matters and investigated intentions by asking more questions in response to participants' words (Bell & Waters, 2014). In doing so I was inspired by Smith, Flowers and Larkin (2009) who suggest that the researcher puts aside her own perceptions of the phenomenon as taken for granted but asks questions and listens to the narrations of participants, while they tell their stories in their own words. This approach contributes to the uniqueness of each transcript, whilst also ensuring that the schedule topics are covered.

I am aware that an interview schedule is merely a guide for the conversation (Biggerstaff & Thompson, 2008), it was not meant to be prescriptive. I was interested in finding out more of their professional life worlds. In other words, I did not want to risk them sharing with me other parts of their life worlds that were irrelevant to my interest. Be that as it may, even though the interview schedule was reduced such that interviews could be completed in an hour, not a single interview out of eight completed was concluded in an hour or less. They all took more than an hour due to the in-depth and rich experiences provided by the psychotherapists. I was cognisant of the time during the interviews but I could not stop the interviews whilst providing rich data that I felt was to be helpful in the study. In most interviews I was asked by participants to finish up because it was time for their next appointments.

Although it is recommended to interview participants twice in order to obtain rich experiences (Harper & Thompson, 2012; Smith & Osborn, 2003), I conducted the interviews once, and substituted the second interview by mailing the transcripts to participants for them to read through and augment any other information they might want to add. This saved time and traveling costs for both myself and participants. It also allowed participants to revisit their interview in a time convenient to each.

Riesmann (2008) says tape recording of dialogues represent what was said in the interview with great precision. I asked participants to sign an audio-recording permission form (see Appendix D) prior the interview, but others signed the forms on the day of the interview. In all cases I was granted permission by my participants to audio-record them. According to Smith and Osborn (2003) audio recording the interview helps in the interviewer focus on the interview process and establishment of rapport with the interviewee rather than focusing on writing interview notes. I used a good quality audio USB recording device (King & Horrocks, 2010). This could then be played on my laptop. My intention was to obtain good quality audio records but in some of interviews there were noises that I did not pick up during the actual recording, which were disturbing during transcription. Moreover, some participants spoke softly so that their voices on the recorder were at times not clearly audible.

According to Willig, 2009 cited in Shinebourne, 2011 after data collation has been completed, individual interviews that were audio recorded are transcribed. IPA necessitates a verbatim transcript of the first-person account (Pietkiewicz & Smith, 2012). Oliver, Serovich and Masson (2005) state that naturalised transcription is a transcription that done in as much detail as possible. The more common structure of the transcript is one prepared as a dramatic script, as if one reads a play. The transcriptions of this study are done in a play-script layout; reading it from top to bottom and left to right. Furthermore, I used a verbatim transcription

(King & Horrocks, 2010), in order to ensure a detailed transcript to assist in the analysis process, to minimise missing out important details that may not seem crucial at the time.

4.5.4 Focus group

A combination of focus groups and individual interviews as data generation methods provide new insights that would have otherwise not surfaced (Barbour & Morgan, 2017). Reid et al (2005) note that focus groups can be used in IPA to collect data. According to Krueger and Casey (2014) focus groups can be composed of five to eight people who have similar experiences or concerns. They discuss a specific issue with the help of a moderator in a particular setting where participants feel comfortable enough to engage in a dynamic discussion for one or two hours (Lianputtong, 2011). Focus groups are formulated to generate data (Morgan, 2018) in order to better understand how people think and/or feel about a phenomenon in a non-threatening environment (Krueger & Casey, 2014). It is the participants that generate data (Morgan, 2018) particularly when they feel comfortable, respected and free to give their opinions without being judged (Krueger & Casey, 2014). Similarities and differences of participants about the phenomenon can be identified in a focus group (Morgan, 2018), thus data is generated further.

During the recruitment stage of this study, I made participants aware that there was going to be a focus group where all participants who were willing, would discuss their recommendations for a way forward. I also discussed that participants would get to see each other in that session and thus their privacy would be compromised. Participants agreed and did not indicate that they had a problem with their privacy being compromised. However, when facilitating the focus group I made sure that I did not indicate who said what during the one on one interview session. In this case, after one-on-one interviews were analysed, a number of themes emerged. This was followed by a focus group where participants discussed these findings in order to ratify what they agreed with, but also to enable participants to broaden on what had emerged, since a second interview with each was not possible (as explained above). In the focus group session I gave participants number tags so they can refer to each other as numbers instead of names or pseudonyms.

4.6 Data analysis

After data has been collected it needs to be analysed for it to make sense or to become knowledge. In this section I discuss the process of analysing data following an IPA paradigm. Pietkiewicz and Smith (2012) suggest emic and etic perspectives in analysing data. The etic style is described as looking at the data using an outsider's lens and interpretation of the participant's experiences; while the emic interpretation of data involves viewing the experiences of the participant, using psychological theories and concepts. Researchers are cautioned not to use theories that are developed in a different setting (Pietkiewicz & Smith, 2012), for example using Western theories to analyse African experiences.

I had three columns in my transcripts. On the left hand side I wrote emic interpretations, in the middle I had the actual transcript, which had lines numbered for ease of cross-referencing. Then in the right hand column I made etic interpretations that were further away from participant's words, in other words interpretations as from an outsider where the theories that came to my mind in reading the words.

Transcripts are analysed individually, following the idiographic element of IPA, in other words they were considered one by one; but following the same pattern of analysis. The first step is to read and re-read the text making initial notes. These are wide-raging and unfocused notes which were done in the left margin (Smith, 2003). At this stage of immersing myself in the raw data, I listen to the audio-recorded dialogue whilst reading the transcript (Forrester & Shaw, 2010). Whilst transcribing, I also found myself taking interest and kept on listening to the interview, smiling, marvelling, laughing or nodding my head instead of typing. This added to the long tedious process of transcribing since I had to re-listen to recordings, which took even longer to transcribe. In this process I also found myself coming up with my own suggestions interpreting the data obtained from participants.

Forrester and Shaw (2010) recommend a reflective journal in which to record an audit trail of how raw data was interpreted to generate the results. Since this is a qualitative research project, its analysis adopts an inductive or 'bottom-up' approach where themes are gathered by going back and forth between themes and transcripts until a comprehensive set of themes is established (Creswell, 2014). I kept a reflective journal in order to establish transparency and trustworthiness of my interpretations.

Forrester and Shaw (2010) note that researchers take an active role in the analysis process, because they are people researching other people, we attribute the same assumptions to ourselves as we do to our participants. I took a subjective stance in this study as a way of decolonising the normative western research reporting that has dominated psychology. The researcher is no neutral observer but a research instrument (Bloor & Wood, 2006). Fontana and Frey (1994) state that researchers get into the real conversations with their participants and are empathic and understanding in order to promote honesty, moral soundness and reliability. Because this is my report of what I have gathered from my participants, I took this subjective stance (Harper & Thompson, 2012) to explore meanings of participants' rich lived experiences.

In this case, although the idiographic element of analysis was followed where case by case analysis took place, a number of overlapping experiences of psychotherapists became evident as I progressed. This makes it sometimes difficult to categorise such experiences under one superordinate theme. This refers to the inter-subjectivity and hermeneutically circular nature of this study.

In each case, participants provided parts or aspects of their understandings of uBuntu and these needed to be drawn together in order for the whole to be understood. This is what I was striving to do in this study, I entered the world of my participants, probed their thoughts and enquired about the meaning of their experiences. In that way I entered their personal as well as professional 'life worlds' by making use of my listening and probing skills. In addition, I enquired what my participants were experiencing and their interpretations of their experience. In the same manner, I decoded the meaning of their experiences to come up with my own interpretation of their experiences thus using double-hermeneutics (Smith & Osborn, 2007). During the interviews, I got closer into the world of psychotherapists by asking them about their deeper experiences. Some of these experiences were rather uncomfortable for my participants, as will be shown in my findings.

The following diagram depicts the stages of analysis I used in each transcript of the individual interview:

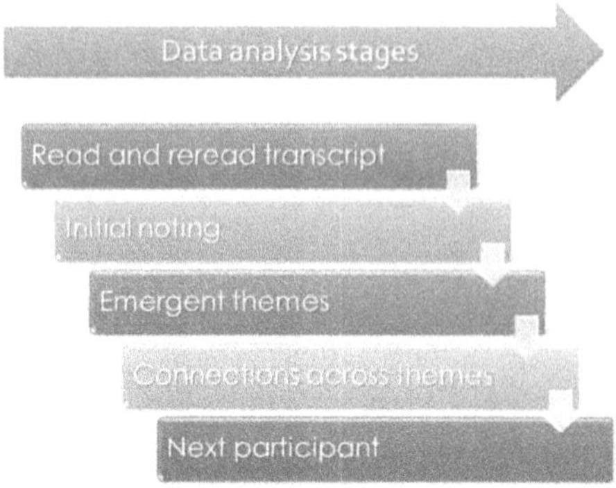

Figure 4.7: Summary of data analysis stages

As illustrated in Figure 4.7 I started by reading and rereading each transcript while listening to the audio. I did my initial noting by writing notes on the transcripts. Then as I became more familiar with their words, I began to synthesise the meanings into emergent themes, a natural cognitive process of condensing meaning. I then made connections across themes and then I moved on to the next transcript.

Smith, Flowers and Larkin (2009) suggests a number of concepts that describe data analysis. One term is abstraction; which is a basic form of identifying patterns between emergent themes and developing a sense of what can be called a superordinate theme. In addition subsumption, although similar to abstraction, functions where an emergent theme itself acquires a super-ordinate status but helps bring together under it a series of related themes. Another term is polarization; which is identifying oppositional relationships between emergent themes. This is done by focusing upon distinctions instead of resemblance. Contextualisation looks at the connections between emergent themes and the environment of the phenomenon to identify contextual or narrative elements within an analysis. Numeration records occurrences where the theme is supported. The function of these different concepts is to assist with the specific purpose of developing emergent themes within the transcript. Following all of this analysis, the researcher can use what makes sense for her in organising themes, showcasing her creativity while also pushing the analysis to a higher level.

4.7 Emergent data

In this study after analysing individual transcripts, in order to identify emergent themes I created a large and comprehensive table where all my participants had a column each with the pseudonym as the heading. Underneath the column of each participant, emergent themes and some descriptions of themes appeared. The far left column was for superordinate themes. The table was my creative manner of bringing it together. The table format made it easier to identify patterns between the emergent themes; which is called abstraction. Moreover, related themes were easily recognised; which Smith, Flowers and Larkin (2009) calls subsumption. In terms of polarisation, within one emergent theme there were sometimes opposing views. This comprehensive table also made it easy to identify how many times a particular emergent theme occurred, thereby facilitating numeration. The final step was to write up my findings, linking examples together to illustrate superordinate and subordinate themes. The following diagram summarises the process I followed to analyse all eight transcripts in order to get to the findings of my study.

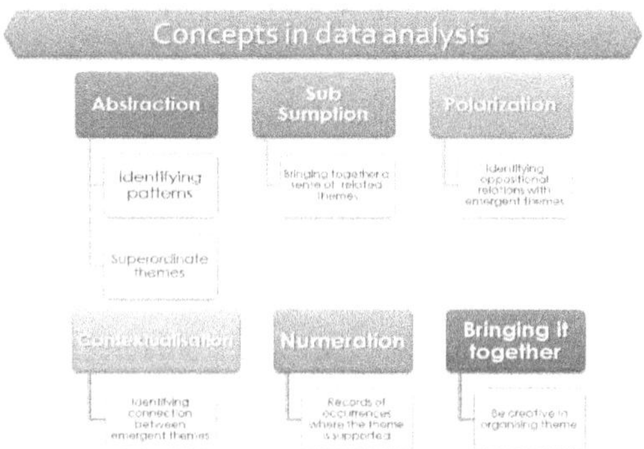

Figure 4.8: Summary of data analysis concepts as derived from Smith et al. (2009)

In this journey of collecting and analysing data I was guided by rules and regulations of research ethics, in order for this study to be deemed authentic and to uphold my integrity as a researcher. The features of these ethical considerations are discussed in the next section.

4.8 Ethics

In the following part, I discuss how I have complied with the HPCSA expectations and those of other relevant ethical bodies in carrying out my researcher duties, in this study. In this regard, Berg (2007) says because social sciences delve into the social lives of other human beings, they have greater ethical obligations, therefore various policies, practices and laws need to be followed. Runswick-Cole (2011) indicates that the interviews involve investigating people's private lives with the aim of describing these experiences publicly, hence the need for ethical care. A number of ethical protocols exist to which the researcher must adhere, when conducting research within health, education and psychology fields.

Proposals to do qualitative projects need to be submitted for ethical review before the project can proceed (Runswick-Cole, 2011). In terms of the South African National Health Act (Act No. 61 of 2003), all health research proposals and protocols require approval by an accredited health research ethics committee before the research may commence (HPCSA, 2008).

In compliance with the above, the proposal for this study was submitted to the department's Research Proposal and Ethical Review Committee (RPERC) and given a tracking number (PSY2015/37) before going to the university's Humanities Higher Degrees Committee (HHDC) for ethical clearance. This was done at the proposal stage before I entered the field. The proposal needed to be approved by HHDC before the field work was underway (see Appendix A).

4.8.1 Confidentiality, anonymity and informed consent

Dunn (2010) defines confidentiality as the right of participant in a research project to keep any personal information private from the public. Berg (2001) also defines confidentiality as an active attempt to eliminate from research any features that might indicate the participant's identity, while anonymity means the participant remains nameless. Runswick-Cole (2011) argues that anonymity and confidentiality are key issues for the researcher particularly at the transcription stage, which must be protected. Report write-ups must ensure confidentiality or anonymity and limitations to confidentiality should be made clear to participants (Banister, et.a., 2011). In this case, I used pseudonyms to protect participants' identities and for anonymity as well as privacy purposes. I did this to ensure that participants' details were excluded from any discussions with my supervisor and the write up of the results. Only the researcher and supervisor had access to any of the raw data. The researcher must ensure that personal information about research participants is collected, stored securely, used and then destroyed. Sometimes during the interview participants would mention their official names but during transcription, I changed their names of the pseudonym, in order to respect their anonymity and confidentiality.

Berg (2007) indicates that informed consent means the individuals know that they are participating in a study and agrees to do so. Participants need to do this as their own free choices and are protected from any element of deceit, duress or similar unfair inducement or manipulation. Dunn (2010) complements this by indicating that persons who are legally adults can give consent and decide whether they want to take part in the research as participants or not. Participants of this study were all adults. In conducting this study I asked participants to voluntarily participate without any unfair inducement or manipulation; as a result some of those psychologists that I asked did not agree to participate and I respected their rights to decline the invitation.

Furthermore, data was stored on a password protected laptop, and backed up on a password protected external hard drive, securely locked away. Over and above these confidentiality, privacy and informed consent measures that I observed, it is important to state that all the participants in this study are registered psychologists who are assumed to be aware of the ethical principles. This means that they are more sensitive to ethical issues than the general public and are thus likely to be more assertive and less vulnerable to being manipulated in any way.

In the following section I discuss more universally accepted research ethical values that I have carefully considered while conducing this study. Such ethical values (Beauchamp & Childress, 2013) are the right to be independent (autonomy), that participants are not exposed to harm (non-maleficence), acting in the best interest of the participants (beneficence), as well as the participants' rights to discontinue.

4.8.2 Autonomy

According to HPCSA (2008) the principle of autonomy means that participants that are capable of deliberation about personal choices should be treated with respect for their capacities of self-determination. They should also be afforded the opportunity to make informed decisions with regard to their participation in research. Therefore there must be special protections for those with diminished or impaired autonomy, not relevant in this instance. In this study I approached and interviewed participants who independently agreed to be participants. They all signed forms agreeing to participate voluntarily. (See Appendix B – Informed consent).

4.8.3 Non-maleficence

According to HPCSA (2008) the principle of non-maleficence must be applied, which means risks and harms of research to participants must be minimised. Bless, Higson-Smith and Sithole (2013) note that the researcher must never harm participants, even unintentionally. In accordance with this principle of non-maleficence, all participants in this study signed informed consent were reassured of the confidentiality clause; and gave permission to audio-tape them before commencement with the interviews (Appendix D). Over and above the fact that participants in this study are all qualified psychologists who wrote the HPCSA board examination before qualifying, which includes ethics; this project was flagged orange by the RPERC, which means that the project contained mild risk. In other words, participants in this study were not considered vulnerable and the study had minimal potential to cause distress, embarrassment or offence to participants. However, I need to be aware of participants' possible concerns about revealing sensitive information.

4.8.4 Acting in the best interest of participants (beneficence)

According to HPCSA (2008) one of the ways of acting in the best interest of participants by the researcher is to be accessible to research participants in the course of investigation. As already mentioned, documents such as informed consent, permission for audio-taping were emailed to participants. This was followed by a phone call to ensure that they received the email and they understood the contents of the email. In the forms sent to participants my and my supervisor's contact details were included. In this way I was accessible to participants. Moreover, if there had been some dissatisfaction or discomfort of some sort by participants, which was caused by me as a researcher, my academic institution or my supervisor was to be informed in order for proper measures to take place.

I concur with Runswick-Cole (2011) who indicates that participants must be made aware of the possible outcomes of participating in the study. At the end of each interview, I explained to participants that the transcripts would be emailed to them so they can add any other information they might wish to. I also explained to them that for their benefit, the outcomes of this study will be shared with them in a form of a focus group before any further dissemination of the findings where we will discuss what to do with the findings of the study.

4.8.5 Discontinuance

Discontinuance means that any participant has the right to terminate participation at any stage in the process of research. In this regard Bless, et al. (2013) confirm that participants must be given assurance that they are free to discontinue without being required to offer explanations. In this research, clause 3 of the consent form (Appendix C) that participants signed included that they are free to discontinue with the study at any given moment without consequences.

4.9 Ensuring research quality

According to Denzin and Lincoln (2008) values for scientific research include internal validity, external validity, replicability and objectivity; which have been criticised as inappropriate for phenomenological enquiry because they relate to positivistic research paradigms. These terms are thus replaced by credibility, transferability, dependability and confirmability (Denzin & Lincoln, 2005), all elements of ensuring trustworthiness. These are discussed in the next section.

4.9.1 Trustworthiness

Trustworthiness is the way the researcher assures her audience that the findings of her study are worth paying attention to. Trustworthiness involves a combination of scientific thinking with human life as lived and conversations among multiple, mutually critical perspectives from different subjectivities and between psychologists and participants: all these relationships are not exclusively privileged (Mouton & Prozesky, 2010).

4.9.1.1 Credibility

According to De Vos (2002) credibility means that the investigation was conducted in such a way that it guarantees that participants were accurately identified and described. In other words, are research findings congruent with the reality as it is experienced by research participants (Toma, 2006)? As I have outlined the process of extracting the findings, to as accurately as possible illustrates what the participants have shared with me and my interpretation of their experiences; as IPA requires. In addition, I sought supervision regularly, especially during the data analysis stage, to ensure that my supervisor agreed with the interpretations that I was making. Furthermore, the return of the findings to the focus group discussion for additional confirmation adds to the levels of credibility achieved.

4.9.1.2 Transferability

Smith et al (2009) argue that theoretical transferability takes place when a reader makes links between the analysis in IPA study, their own personal and professional experiences and contextualised analysis of the accounts of the participants. This enables readers to evaluate its transferability to persons in contexts which are more or less similar. In this case, the literature review highlights that there are other psychotherapists in different environments who may have had similar experiences, and my presentation of these findings at various conference events has also shown that others resonate with the findings. These elements show that there is likely to be some transferability, particularly in the SA context, where psychotherapists are working with people who ascribe to concepts related to uBuntu.

4.9.1.3 Dependability

According to Lincoln & Guba (1985) dependability looks at the consistency of the research findings with data collected. In other words, can the study be replicated should it be repeated with the same participants in the same context? In this case I have given as many details about the process as possible and followed the IPA style of doing research. These factors strive to ensure that the study is dependable.

4.9.1.4 Confirmability

Confirmation means the results can be confirmed by another researcher (Dunn, 2010). This means that the findings of an investigation conducted by a researcher, when repeated by another researcher will lead to similar findings as the first (McCready in Leong & Austin, 2006). However, Seale, Gobo, Gubrium and Silverman (2004) argue that to check findings may be limited by contextual influences, thus making findings more particular.
To conclude, I have hopefully illustrated the trustworthiness of this qualitative study as best I can. It is equally important to argue that these were supported by the triangulation process the study followed, as discussed in the next section.

4.9.2 Triangulation

Creswell (2007) indicates that triangulation involves using multiple methods, data sources, observers, or theories in order to gain a more complete understanding of the phenomenon being studied, in order to ensure robust, rich, comprehensive, and well-developed research findings. Berg (2007) adds that triangulation is the use of multiple lines of sight, for researchers to obtain a better more substantive picture of reality; to lead to symbols and concepts as a means of verifying many of these elements. In this case data source triangulation was used, where multiple participants from different locations and categories of psychology were interviewed on the same topic to ensure a more in-depth understanding of their experiences and to identify similarities in their accounts.

Different authors throughout this study are referenced to explain and verify relevant concepts. Besides my supervisor who confirms that this study is current and relevant; (as noted above), I have presented this study in multiple workshops and conferences, where different scholars from humanities and social sciences of many South African and most Sub-Saharan countries' universities were represented, its relevance to their work was confirmed. To add, my participants also took part in this study because they thought it was going to contribute to the decolonising of psychology, which is a very current topic of debate in the profession.

4.9.2.1 Member checking

Creswell (2014) indicates that member checking is used to determine the accuracy of the qualitative findings through taking the final report or specific descriptions or themes back to participants and determining whether these participants feel that they are accurate. In this case I started by emailing each transcript back to each participant, in order for the participant to indicate whether the transcript was a true reflection of what they shared. Some additions were made by email whereas others did not have any more information to add. As already indicated, in a focus group I also shared findings with participants. This process further allowed participants to clarify what their intentions were, to correct any errors, and provide additional information, if necessary.

4.10 Conclusion: Ethical responsibility of the researcher

Bless, et al. (2013) indicate that should researchers fail to comply with ethics they may be censored by their professional bodies or they may be dismissed by their employers or they may be prosecuted by research participants. Additionally, researchers have responsibilities of relevance which means researchers should aim to make a useful contribution to society. In this case, judging by the responses and excitement that I get from scholars when I present this study in conferences, I am hopeful that it will make a meaningful contribution to the developing democratic South Africa with an approach to psychotherapy that is more decolonised and thus having greater relevance to the people.

Moreover, in terms of promulgation of results, researchers have the responsibility to make their findings available in a form that is usable by people who can benefit from them (Bless et al, 2013). This means that researchers must find other ways to make their findings known. I have already discussed my findings with my participants and the copy of my thesis will be a public document kept in the Rhodes University library in Makhanda (formerly Grahamstown) and an electronic copy will also be available on line. Finally, I have already received invitations to publish the findings of this research, a task I wish to pursue on conclusion of this write-up.

To summarise, this is a qualitative research that has undertaken a phenomenological enquiry and has implemented IPA for analyses. I have followed all the necessary steps to conduct this type of research and have hopefully stated clearly how I have followed such steps.

In conclusion, in this chapter I have discussed the umbrella methodology of this study and IPA, the specific phenomenological analysis taken in this study. I also discussed how IPA has influenced how I have conducted this study. I discussed recruitment and sampling, and how data was collected by making use of interviews and a focus group. I concluded by discussing how the resultant data was analysed and my care in the application of ethics throughout these processes.

CHAPTER 5

FINDINGS

"It's part of me... How can I separate myself from it?"

The aim of this study is to investigate psychotherapists' experiences regarding the incorporation of principles of uBuntu in their practice. Moreover, it is to understand the lived experiences and dilemmas of psychotherapists who engage with uBuntu practices in their psychotherapy as well as to interpret how participants make sense of such. This is a long chapter so I decided that dividing it into 'chewable chunks' would make it more 'palatable'. In this I am inspired by Smith, Flowers and Larkin (2009) who say that bringing data together means that a researcher uses what works for them, showcasing their creativity while pushing the analysis to a higher level. I divided this chapter into two parts, namely part A and part B. Part A refers to the superordinate themes derived from raw data, while part B is about uBuntu. In both parts I respond to the research questions indicated in chapter 3.

PART A: Themes

After I had analysed data, a collection of findings that capture the phenomenological sense of experiences were categorised as follows. Categories are not totally exclusive, so there is likely to be some overlap. Five superordinate themes were identified including socialisation factors, adherence to psychotherapy principles, therapy frames adjustments, influences of uBuntu on certain practice issues and lastly suggestions for psychotherapy expansions. These superordinate themes will each be explored below and are summarised in figure 5.1 below:

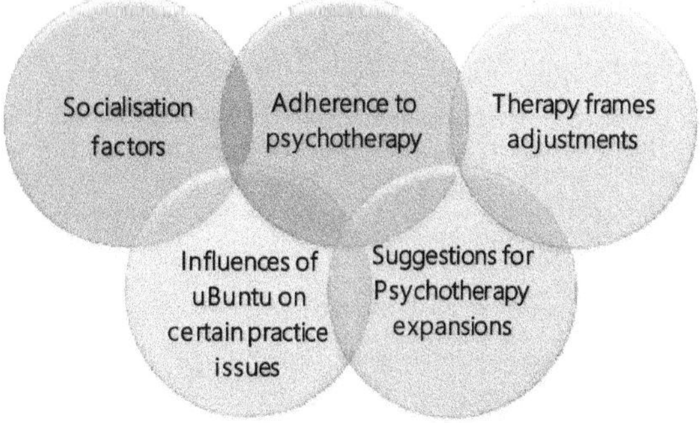

Figure 5.1: Summary of findings derived from the raw data

These superordinate themes each have subordinate themes which will also be deliberated on in this chapter. This part of the chapter responds to research question 1, namely 'What are the original principles and ethics of psychotherapy and how do these cause dissonance among psychotherapists that are of African origin?'

5.1 Socialisation factors

Socialisation factors were deduced from thick descriptions of participants. Language, gender issues, isiXhosa traditions and poor socioeconomic backgrounds became prevalent as subordinate themes under socialisation factors. The impact of amaXhosa socialisation on behaviours are described below, which influences the processes of psychotherapy.

5.1.1 Language and culture

It would seem that most people prefer to express themselves in their vernacular; hence amaXhosa clients choose isiXhosa-speaking psychotherapists. They can express themselves without the concern that they are not being understood by someone who does not speak their language. In addition, both the client and the psychotherapist are socialised in aspects of the amaXhosa worldview; which deepens the understanding of the language.

In the case of psychotherapy, speaking isiXhosa in sessions appears to speed up rapport; clients become comfortable in that they find something in common between the psychotherapist and themselves. In this regard, P1 said:

> *I have been working mostly with isiXhosa speaking clients; ..., because of issues of language and all that. Because most students come from rural areas, they are limited in English, they are not English speakers. They would feel comfortable to come and talk to me, expressing themselves in their own language. Sometimes language can be a barrier to people who do not speak the language.*

P1 notes that some people have a limited command of English, due to little exposure; and is thus identifying language difficulties as a potential barrier in psychotherapy. Since speaking in isiXhosa in the sessions transcends to other areas of living such as traditional cultural practices, it promotes a better understanding between the psychotherapist and the client. P8 reported:

Language is very important and the fact that I was Xhosa speaking but later I realised that it translated also to the issues of culture that people would bring and which issues were also addressed by traditional healers or diviners that line of people.

While P1 also indicated:

...also culturally I understand them when they talk about issues that are happening at home, like 'amasiko' (rituals) *and all that. Sometimes those issues come in this practise and I am able to actually listen to those and understand them better.*

Both participants thus refer particularly to spiritual elements related to healers or rituals.

Although most people find comfort in expressing themselves in their vernacular, times and culture are not static. A psychotherapist based in a university indicated that although she works with more Black clients she noticed that most of them speak English even those that are amaXhosa. This is partly due to the influence of some students attending schools, where English predominates amongst learners. P5 said about the language she uses in psychotherapy:

isiXhosa, isiXhosa mostly and mix you know moss amaXhosa always 'Xenglish'.

'Xenglish' is a term used for mixing isiXhosa and English. This means that amaXhosa in the more urbanised areas where interviews were conducted mostly mix isiXhosa and English when they converse.

P4 added to the above, noting adaptability to the clients' preferences

I use isiXhosa mostly but of course you will find that in most cases some of our kids are more comfortable in English so I think I take whatever the child comes with and adapt into that.

Participants indicated that they allow their clients to choose the language to be used in psychotherapy. All of the participants interviewed were at least bilingual in both isiXhosa and English.

5.1.2 Gender issues

For amaXhosa males raised in a patriarchal way, attending psychotherapy is interpreted as something more suited to women. For most, being seen to seek assistance implies being unable to handle their own problems. amaXhosa males are socialised not to talk about their problems, particularly to strangers. In most practices therefore, it is mostly females that consult. P1said:

> *Most of the time counselling is a new concept to men, talking to a stranger is a new concept to them.*

Participants indicated that they mostly see females as their clients. P1 summarised what most of my participants said.

> *I see Blacks, age varies ... most of the time it's females you know, that I would see, yes there were males but it's females mostly.*

For amaXhosa it is believed that men do not talk about their problems. A well-used saying is '*Indod'ayikhali' (*men do not cry), which can be translated as: a male sharing his troubles, frustrations or any emotional turmoil, is perceived as someone who is crying. Crying is interpreted as a sign of weakness.

5.1.3 amaXhosa traditions

Psychotherapy is fairly 'new' as a practice, especially since access to it was very limited prior to democracy. As noted in 5.1.1, amaXhosa are used to ways of healing that include traditional healers or diviners. Nowadays some of those ways of healing are seen as backwards and witchcraft- associated, due to acculturation and modernised healing interventions. This makes people consult with such healers more secretly. As a result, to actually talk about them takes a lot of courage. P1 commented:

> *I think the reason why he trusted it, changed it, is because I did not judge him and say that the thing you went to is not going to work, it is nonsense and it is not going to work, it is not scientific. It is his belief system it is how he grew up and he believes in it, so I think that is why he continued with me.*

P1 notes above that the client continued consulting due to the non-judgemental approach taken, respecting the belief system of the client

5.1.4 Poor socio-economic backgrounds

As indicated in chapter 1 amaXhosa mostly live in the Eastern Cape Province which is the largest and the poorest province in SA. The socio-economic status of people influences the

way people are socialised. In order for people to survive in poverty situations they need to behave in a communal way so that when they have a need it can be met by their neighbours or relatives who might have access to better resources at the time. For example, when they lack such commodities as sugar, bread and so on, a neighbour can share with them.
Under normal circumstances psychotherapy should be about the issues that are psychologically troubling the client; but due to the South African context, where Blacks are predominantly poor and mostly lack basic needs, psychotherapists find themselves helping clients in ways that go beyond their psychotherapeutic roles. Both the psychotherapist and the client are socialised as amaXhosa to assist where needed. P2 explained this further, including what she finds most challenging about the situation:

> A *student* [client]*coming all the way for whatever they come from, they do not have money to pay for their accommodation, they don't have money for food, they don't have food meanwhile they must sit in a lecture and listen and focus and absorb and understand. Then you call the Dean of students. Sometimes students cannot be helped. They would leave their homes with nothing, leaving their grandmother who is only getting grant from the government and that is their sole source of income, for me that's the most difficult. You help where you can.*

Participants feel that sharing some resources they have with their clients is helpful to clients. They sometimes refer their clients to places where they can be supported financially or with food, such as the department of social development. That is the extra help they give to their clients and they are socialised to assist where they are able to.

Due to different socio-economic backgrounds of psychotherapists in practice, people have different experiences. P7 indicated:

> *You must also remember that we are all psychologists Black and white. We are coming from the same conditions but social, political and economic conditions, we are not. Certain thing in our scope of practise would limit other people for them and to get our services and for us to do certain things to our clients not because what you will be doing is wrong, it will be wrong across the board. It does not actually look at the conditions like the client condition; it says that the scope of practice will say you must comply with ethics.*

In other words, the rules or policies regulating psychotherapy are meant to be applied by all practitioners, regardless of their backgrounds and clientele. What is unethical for practitioners who work with clients who can pay for services is also then viewed as unethical for practitioners who work with those clients that come from predominantly poor socio-economic backgrounds. However, in the latter cases, psychotherapy becomes a secondary need where a primary need is a basic need such as food.

Sometimes the dilemma psychotherapists find themselves in is influenced by the rules, regulations and ethics of psychology that do not seem to be clear. This further responds to research question 1: What are the original principles and ethics of psychotherapy and how do these cause dissonance among psychotherapists that are of African origin? In such cases a psychotherapist is faced with the responsibility of making decisions about each case. P7 continued:

> *Where my client is coming from, why will I not extend my services and consider the economic issues of my client which the scope of practise is silent about? So I am using my own discretion.*

We as amaXhosa psychotherapists find ourselves in a dilemma when we know how we supposedly ought to practice, but the realities we are faced with force us to go against our training background for humanitarian reasons and what we know is ethically expected of us, and use what is helpful for our clients. P7 thus further expressed frustration:

> *But ...I was taught that you don't go visit, just make phone calls ask them to come here in my office, the whole family doesn't have money how do you expect them to come here but if I go there what a difference it makes if I go there. To me uBuntu is to go an extra mile you know go against what you were taught, sometimes.*

P1 uses her discretion about cases involving poor socio-economic status of clients. This has led her finding herself sharing her resources with clients. She indicated:

> *... you know you want to help, but there are sometimes boundaries. I gave that person a R100 just to go home because he had been here and just to make a difference, even if it is just for the day.*

In this case the psychotherapist may seem to be stepping well beyond her therapeutic role and setting up conditions of undue dependency; however, as a caring person with no other social services resources to turn to, she feels compelled to assist in the best way she can at that point. After all, the essence of psychotherapy is a helping profession. P1 gave client money to buy food for her, she explained further:

> *Ndamnika, (I gave her) Yes, I gave it [*money*] to her. Ndathatha ishort cut egameni lobuntu (I took a shortcut in the name of uBuntu).*

In this case it is the psychotherapist that gives gifts to clients. The practitioner saw an urgent need to assist a client but also acknowledges that this was a 'short cut'; showing that she was aware that she might have done something else, such as a referral onwards if this had been possible, but she responds out of her compassion, which she ascribes to uBuntu. Psychotherapy is meant to be about imparting skills to client to be independent. In other words psychotherapy is designed to 'teach people how to fish instead of fishing for people, but in this case. P1 fished for the client. She was quite aware that she was not supposed to act as such.

A further example was given by P7 as follows:

> *I have given a client a bus fare, look my practise is situated in a suburb and these clients are coming from the location, they really need to see me but they do not have bus fare, how do you expect me?*

The issue of affordability may hinder the effectiveness of psychotherapy in circumstances where there is a considerable distance between the psychologist's office 'in a suburb' and where the client lives, in a township on the outskirts of town known as a 'location'. P7 in the above quote acted from the spirit of uBuntu by providing bus fare for the client; and at the same time psychotherapy took place.

The above are some of the experiences and dilemmas that are facing amaXhosa psychotherapists in their practises. This may be due to the fact that the very same psychotherapists also come from experiences of the same socio-economic backgrounds as their clients. This is a dilemma, because the traditional way of practising psychotherapy discourages practitioners from behaving as such. However, in the spirit of uBuntu; a person with resources is expected to assist the less privileged by sharing those resources.

Dissonances that are facing psychotherapist due to their background as amaXhosa and their Western practice continue to happen as noted in the following section. These dissonances may be as a result of psychotherapists trying to comply with the rules of conducting psychotherapy as per their training. The second superordinate theme of findings is adherence to psychotherapy principles.

5.2 Adherence to psychotherapy principles

The following diagram is the summary of a theme that I have called adherence to psychotherapy which has subordinate themes as illustrated.

Figure 5.2: Sub-themes that identify principles accepted by participants

Both psychotherapist and client need to be protected from harm, therefore there must be guidelines or rules of doing psychotherapy. In practice, participants were very aware of these, but also expanded on the challenges as they became more experienced. P6 reported:

> *...I used to really adhere to rules when I started but from my experience .... I would like psychotherapy or that relationship to be human to human, I feel like we can be in a same box with the do's and don'ts ... I would like it to be a natural flow of a relationship.*

P6 was implying that sticking to the rules intimidates certain clients and brings about an element of anxiety. She would like to practise in such a way that a psychotherapist is perceived as someone who has a comfortable relationship with clients that is not anxiety triggering. Her experience in psychotherapy taught her to be more natural in sessions than being mindful of rules all the time.

Participants noted that there is no allowance made for different cultures or backgrounds, in terms of applying principles of psychotherapy to practise. P7 indicated the tension between doing what is judged to be morally correct and following HPCSA policies:

> *…not because what you will be doing is wrong, it will be wrong because of the scope of practice that is written across the board. It does not actually look at the conditions like the client's conditions... you must do policy... you must make sure you make an individual counselling using the modalities you were trained in ...*

As much as adhering to psychotherapy principles is the right thing to do, it potentially also restricts psychotherapists from applying themselves fully in the sessions because they have to be mindful of what they must not do. Sometimes they have a dilemma where they are not sure of what to do since the ethical codes do not make allowances for differences in client backgrounds. One of the sub-themes of adherence to psychotherapy principles relate to access to the process.

5.2.1 Entry points to psychotherapy

This refers to the source of referrals for psychotherapy. As implied above, psychotherapy is costly and most people that come from poor socio-economic backgrounds cannot afford such services. This section refers to how clients then access the service. P7 said:

> *... Black doctors, Xhosa speaking doctors... they usually send people to me, sometimes my colleague sends them to me, if it is not children that she sees*

P3 added to the list of people that normally refer clients.

> *... referred to me by ICAS* [a Wellness Company] *word of mouth, people that I have helped already, doctors, schools.*

It seems that referrals to psychotherapists are mostly made by specific professionals or people that have also benefited from psychotherapy services. This implies that psychologists must be known as practitioners in order to get referrals.

As a way of introducing themselves to the public, psychotherapists may do volunteer work in groups, without remuneration. P1 shared:

> *I even tell them in those sessions when I have those group sessions .... when you go for therapy, when you go for counselling because some of them also believe that if you come for counselling you must be someone who is mentally challenged.*

This means that she works in groups to explain to potential clients how psychological services function and in the process alleviates misconceptions about psychotherapy. After such group sessions clients may then start to make appointments for psychotherapy.

In certain academic institutions, identifying psychotherapy clients becomes a concerted effort between the academic staff members and psychotherapists. Referrals in such instances are also from the group work that is provided. P1 continued:

> *I formulate group sessions according to their lecturers. Lecturers because they interact with students every day, they identify students in that class. They will send me those groups of students.*

Working with clients who come from poor socio-economic backgrounds is sometimes a challenge. Psychotherapists work voluntarily in order to get referrals of clients who would hopefully pay for their services. It is an uBuntu gesture to volunteer and see clients who do not pay, but psychotherapists have bills to pay. This means it takes time for their practise to become fully-fledged as opposed to others who work with clients that pay. This may mean that Black psychotherapists may have to find other means of topping up income. Marketing, which is prohibited by the ethical guidelines of the HPCSA, may assist in making psychotherapists known by the public. In this case adhering to psychotherapy principles could be detrimental to psychotherapists wishing to attract clients through the provision of information.

5.2.2 Privacy and informed consent

Psychotherapy is designed in such a way that privacy of individuals is protected. The traditional way of conducting psychotherapy is in behind closed doors with a note ‘do not disturb' on the other side of the door, and in rooms that are sound proof if possible. Added to privacy is deep respect for others; which informs our desires for people to give informed consent, based clearly on understanding the process. Although in amaXhosa traditional communications and relationships there is no emphasis on privacy and informed consent, participants reported that in psychotherapy privacy seems crucial also for amaXhosa clients. P6 indicated:

> *... we have to be rigid about the person's privacy...*

P8 echoed the above sentiments.

> *I still feel that therapy should happen in closed spaces, secluded so to speak, they take place between the therapist and the client, that sort of setting...*

For example, P2 did not feel comfortable doing psychotherapy in hospitals, she reported:

> *... I do not like the idea of me standing over a person, it felt odd I mean they do not give you privacy and they do not have sessional rooms for instance, ...I would rather wait for the person to actually get a little bit better...*

It is apparent that psychotherapists want to preserve privacy and informed consent as part of their ethical practice. These two ethical guidelines are reportedly effective for participants and appear to work well with amaXhosa clients although they originated from the west. Therefore, adhering to psychotherapy principles regarding privacy and informed consent seems beneficial to the amaXhosa client, psychotherapists and the process.

5.2.3 Rapport, hugs and touching clients

Rapport can be created in different ways: amaXhosa have a way of establishing their rapport which may be different from the Western way. P7 commented:

> *At first it was difficult because of how I was taught at the university ... be careful of hugging, be careful of this and this and this; for me it's nothing because I work with people who wants to be touched, you know Black blood like Xhosa speaking ..., to me it is a rapport on its own to shake hands to give you a hug it is a rapport, to hold a boy in his fore head is a rapport; so those kind of gestures can be used to strengthen your rapport with your client but I know from the Black particularly they hug .... To*

me it is another way of creating a rapport I show my client that I trust you and if your fundamentals in your therapy if it lacks trust you have lost that client.

From P7's perspective, it is evident that the rule about not touching a client at all would disturb the meeting phase and might very well alienate the client, detracting from building any rapport. Some practical ways of building rapport include seating posture, tone of voice, eye contact and displaying warmth and caring. P7 also reported:

> *... that creating a rapport I think that it cuts through all the modalities of frameworks that we use; one would have to create a good rapport from the onset and also try to use certain concepts from that modality we use or framework we use.*

This means rapport building with clients is foundational to all theoretical approaches and therefore crucial part of psychotherapy.

The naturally occurring touching among amaXhosa including the shaking hands, hugs and touching to comfort seems to be important as reported by the participants and seems to indicate acceptance of one another. It seems to overlap with the interconnectedness that is one of the core principles of uBuntu to be explored further below. As illustrated above, psychotherapists are thus faced with a dilemma of touching or not touching clients. In every interaction, compassion involves touching and hugging the other, this means acceptance, love and caring. Hugging and handshakes are common amongst amaXhosa, even with strangers; denoting the humanity of each other.

This is also illustrative of the dilemmas between the actual practice with amaXhosa and what is professionally expected of practitioners. Sometimes clients hug or extend their hand for a handshake first. P2 shared her two experiences:

> *... this one client was so excited at the end of the session she stood up and hugged me and I did not say no, ... this child was ecstatic, happy that she made it through the session...*

In this case a hug was a sign of relief or of excitement because of some breakthrough achieved during the session. In other cases psychotherapists follow the lead of the client. In this regard P8 reported:

... I shake their hands if they bend to hug me I hug them so I do not have a problem with that, I do not feel that there is intimacy, ... if you do not do you do not show warmth, perhaps you showing coldness and distance. So what is your choice to be perceived as cold and distant or you rather be perceived as warm and welcoming. ... I do not matter more than the client here, so what the client does I do.

Even though P8 is client-centred he is aware and careful of rules preventing intimacies and tensions created by these when one needs to show compassion. In other words, it is understood that in some cases touching and hugging clients may not be for establishing rapport but may be for intimate reasons; which are prohibited by psychotherapy guidelines for non-maleficence purposes. P8 continued:

So I am both a human being, but I am also a therapist so I have not been bribed by those hugs and although the client might have wished that they could have bribed me, but if they wanted me to be bribed by them then they would not have come here.

Here, the participant is indicating the need for therapists to take care not to be deceived if hugs are used by clients to convey a message other than a greeting, but the last part seems to discount such occurrences. Overall these quotes show how using culturally appropriate touch serves a number of purposes, but chiefly compassion seems to be indicated.

5.2.4 Confidentiality

It would seem that although certain Eurocentric principles of psychotherapy do not sit well with amaXhosa psychotherapists, some are valued and preserved even though they have been adopted from Western approaches, including confidentiality. P6 noted:

...there are those we have to be rigid about like confidentiality...

P8 added:

I always remind them that the things we speak about here are spoken in confidence and they are between the two of us, on threshold, nothing goes out, nothing comes in, yeah! So we have confidence understanding but it is also, you know, the law that it be done that way.

To conclude the theme of adherence, confidentiality, respect and privacy seem to be the values that amaXhosa psychologists seem to want to preserve in psychotherapy. On the other hand, although establishing rapport seems to be important, but it is established differently in amaXhosa psychotherapy. Another superordinate theme is the therapy frame and participants suggestions for adjustments as discussed in the next section.

5.3 Therapy frame adjustments

Therapy frames are ground rules of psychotherapy that are not as rigid as ethics. They are more accommodative and they do not pose harm or threat to either the client or therapist. These therapy frames also known as boundaries include a safe private space for seeing clients, which psychotherapists indicated they want to preserve. P5 indicated her understanding of therapy frames as:

> *Ground rules in my understanding. They are about boundaries, boundaries of time like one of the things I discuss with the client before we start we've got an hour I usually say 5 minutes before the end sometimes if you just have the clock we can go over time so I said that "I'll let you know it's about the boundaries in terms of time"... I tell them the way I was trained I'm not supposed to interact with you because people may ask 'oh where do you know the psychologist '?...*

The above show both awareness of adhering to time limits and also refers to not having contact in social settings to protect the client. Psychotherapists are trained to be mindful of psychotherapy frames but sometimes psychotherapists find it difficult to observe such frames due to circumstances that are beyond their control. P4 indicated:

> *...you meet someone out of the therapy room and they want to talk about their child and I will find that in as much as I know that we are not supposed to be discussing this, but if I realize that she is in a state that she wants to share something with me I will give that moment, I will give her that time I will accommodate that even thou I know that even ethically for that matter we should not be discussing therapeutic things outside of therapeutic space...*

The above extract is an illustration of the circumstances where a therapist in not in a position to dictate the behaviour of the client. In other words, although the psychotherapists want to use private and safe space for psychotherapy, clients sometimes do not comply. In this case ignoring a client on the basis that it is not within the boundaries of psychotherapy space could be more harmful to the client than the discomfort that the psychotherapist may feel. Making sense of this behaviour displayed by clients P4 continues:

> *I think maybe by virtue of, I don't know me being me you know, or knowing sometimes people don't always think of you as they know at the back of their minds that you are a psychologist, but they do not think of you in that sense they look at you and they feel that you are someone comfortable they want to talk to, telling their problems to so they don't feel that they have to come to your office to talk about things they can talk to you anywhere.*

This participant seems infer that, this behaviour displayed by clients may be reflective of a good, positive and comfortable relationship between the client and the therapist. However, some psychotherapists feel obliged to adhere to strict boundaries, P2 reported:

> *...I am very much mindful of the boundaries, I'm very much careful about creating precedence, I don't like to do things that I will not be able to carry over...I am so much about creating those boundaries...*

Although the above two showed knowledge, most of my participants did not know what the therapy frames were during the interview. I had to expand on the question most of the time. This means that the natural focus of most participants was mostly on the ethics that were punishable by law or professionally. It would seem as if even though psychotherapists kept some ground rules, it was their clients who seemed not to be aware of these. This again illustrates the dilemmas faced by amaXhosa psychotherapists, as expanded in examples below.

5.3.1 African time

'African time' is a phenomenon which is displayed by Africans about a more relaxed attitude towards time. Some of the lived experiences of psychotherapists regarding the therapeutic hour when working with amaXhosa clients involve this phenomenon. The psychotherapy hour, according to the Board of Health Funders is 50 to 60 minutes. Most participants indicated that in their practice this traditional hour is not always practical, for psychotherapists who practise uBuntu, the extra minutes will not be charged. P4 indicated:

… that is very challenging and we get that quite often to be honest with you. In the beginning I really struggled with that and I get very upset but I came to a stage where I decided in giving people information and they needed to know that they have an hour and if they come at 11h15 we will stop at 12h00 so the more we gave people information the more I felt comfortable that I do not have to give extra time for someone who came late and we start the session and stop at 12h00, but then that is not always practical. ... sometimes the content of therapy of the session will dictate if you will actually stop at 12h00 because sometimes the session is so intense that is a lot of emotions within the session and like I mean you cannot look at the clock and say it is 12h00 we have to wrap up, you have to give the person sort of time to calm down and contain themselves...

As noted above, this poses a dilemma to a psychotherapist who is trained in a traditional Western worldview but comes from the 'African time' background. Psychotherapists are inconvenienced by the 'African time' phenomenon but feel the need to justify why they cannot comply with this phenomenon. However, some psychologists seem to have adjusted to this phenomenon when working with amaXhosa clients. In this regard P6 reported:

I have other people to see so we should be having a starting time, if a person comes late we will use the time that is left for the session. Like I do not become hysterical there is a starting time, but when the client is late, we start when he arrives.

This means that the participant adapted herself to 'African time' in her practice. This may be due to her acknowledging that coming late to sessions by clients is a habit of living that is not going to improve easily. Sometimes however, 'African time" is influenced by the client's impoverished socio-economic background. P7 explained:

… so I've got a ruling in my practice that if you arrive late after 15 minutes you are not going to get a full hour you'll be getting 45 minutes and if you arrive after 30 minutes, I will see you but not more than that hour you know and I discuss that in the first session..., 'eish' you know we are Xhosas... sometimes it doesn't work and doesn't always work in this way, I understand that they are taking taxis and they are out of their control and it is out of my control...

The 'eish' above is an exclamation reflective of stress caused by confusion of the dilemma. The above quotes hint at the need for practitioners to try not to get stressed about exact time-keeping. As illustrated 'African time' in certain situations may be caused by reasons beyond the client's control. For example, in the case when the client comes for sessions late maybe due to taxi challenges, over and above the time issue, the psychotherapist finds himself doing more than expected. P7 continued:

> *I cannot just leave that person so I will extend time, because of this case is like a hot potatoes you know this person really needs my attention, it's not something you can suspend and come back the following day...*

This means the participant feels the responsibility of assisting a fellow human being who seems to be experiencing life challenges.

'African time' forms part of the context in which amaXhosa psychotherapists work and therefore it may be beneficial for them to acknowledge that it is a phenomenon they need to live with; but as noted above, some practitioners do not address the issue with clients and explain the potential time constraints they need to work within. When adjustments are made, this highlights psychotherapists' humanity, compassion, understanding and selflessness.

5.3.2 Advice giving

Western psychology discourages practitioners from giving advice to clients. Instead of giving advice you explore options and allow the client to choose what the client thinks and feels will be the best for him or her. In traditional amaXhosa practice a more knowledgeable person will give advice to the younger. In most cases, clients expect to come to psychotherapy to receive advice. This illustrates another dilemma that is faced by amaXhosa practising psychotherapists P1 reported:

> *Because most of them* (clients) *don't know what to expect for counselling, but you will have those after like you explained ... says "kengoku ndithini"* – (And now what must I do?)" *'Ndimbon'uba uyademander',* (I will perceive him/her as demanding). *I will explain to them, sometimes I become uncomfortable in giving advices, because my fear is that it might backfire and sometimes you might not have resources internal resources to implement my advice because we are two different people.*

P1 finds herself under pressure from clients who are demanding to be given advice by her even though she would have covered in the introduction session that her role is not to give advice but to work with the client to find solutions to her problems. Giving advice to clients contradicts with how psychology must be practised. Psychotherapists are discouraged from giving advice to clients but clients feel that they are not receiving adequate service from their psychotherapists should they not be given advice in their sessions. Sometimes amaXhosa psychotherapists find themselves advising clients due to the pressure they receive from them. After giving advice they feel the need to justify why they gave advices in those instances. In this regard P7 said:

> *... particularly when it comes to abusive cases the most physical abuse, emotional abuse, I find myself giving advice, if you are being abused at home you don't know what to do it is not easy for me to ask what do you think, I just say hey sister, hey brother go to the police and most of cases it actually leads me to give recommendations immediately and advice.*

In amaXhosa culture '*inyathi ibuzwa kwabaphambili*' (you get a direction from the people who have travelled the route/road before), in other words people who have experience or who are in authority will be able to give you direction or guidance. P8 indicated:

> *They were drawing from the culture_and therefore to be a traditional healer would mean the wisest person in culture things or a person who is endowed with those special powers of religion and so on.*

When people visit such healers, they are told what to do, and expect the same when visiting a psychologist. This poses some dilemmas that to amaXhosa psychotherapists including doing what is expected by clients and what is professionally expected due to Western rules for conducting psychotherapy. Complying with the rules sometimes fails clients as their expectations are different. For example, P5 reported:

> *Because I usually ask you know about their expectations, they say oh that you give me advice. Of course I explain that I do not give advice and I tell them why I cannot give them advice, why I cannot give them advice because I ask a client what's your understanding of you being here seeing a psychologist?*

This has a dual meaning: firstly, the psychotherapist exercised his ethical responsibility to give direction to the participant to report to the relevant services in such cases. Secondly the therapist is appropriately giving advice and influencing the client to do what the therapist feels the client needs to do in order that the client is not harmed further.

This shows that the participant tries to explain how she works, but clients expect to be told what to do in different situations. P5 continued:

> *And sometimes that is when I have to correct to say you know I will not be giving you advice and explain what I mean by that why am I not going to give advice.*

This participant due to their training, comply with the not giving of advice, although they feel pressure from clients' expectations. This giving advice is the 'rule' that they appear to resist although people do perhaps subtly give advice through the directions of their questions or reflections.

Another subtheme for adjusting psychotherapy frames indicated by participants eschews rigidity and encourages flexibility.

5.3.3 Flexibility

As much as psychotherapy needs to change in order to accommodate people with whom it is practised, psychotherapists need to acknowledge that times progress and culture is not static and thus apply some flexibility in their practise. In this regard P5 reported:

> *That's why I'm saying flexibility, yes its part of uBuntu not really cut off a person like that, even if the time is up if you know that this is at a critical time you really want to help the person or contain the person; like as I say there's a notification that ok our time is coming to an end but sometimes depends there's a circumstance if somebody coming in later I don't want a person to wait for 30 minutes while she has an appointment but maybe it's 5 minutes ok let's just extend a little bit*

Flexibility is an important feature for psychotherapists. P5 also said:

> *I believe one of the characteristics of what as a therapist you need to be flexible. So even if a person I explain to a person if I finish today I would like to see you for the next session but if a person has got a problem and they cannot make it I can shift them to another day so I do that flexibility around the time ja...*

Flexibility recognises that human beings are not perfect beings. Such imperfections may influence the way psychotherapists practice such as adhering to rigid times. Flexibility is also needed in not making judgements or jumping to conclusions about certain behaviours displayed by people. In this regard P7 said:

> *I am coming from a school of thought where they say you don't look at a person in the eye because is a sign of disrespect, now that it is changing particularly those people are coming for sessions they look at you and would I interpret that as being a disrespect, no times change...*

This quote refers to some amaXhosa ways of behaviour that differ from the traditional western behaviours. In amaXhosa traditions looking a person in the eye is perceived as disrespectful. However, as indicated above, things and times change, psychotherapists therefore need to change with times and be flexible in their approach.

Sometimes attending sessions for certain clients may be difficult, flexibility therefore in order to accommodate and encourage people to make use of the services becomes crucial. P1 shared:

> *I'm also flexible ... one will say I came to see you (meaning this is a casual visit) ... I was checking if you were available... it ends up being a session*

This is one of the dilemmas experienced by amaXhosa psychotherapists. Sometimes clients do not follow the protocol of rescheduling sessions because they feel they just want to talk and to them one does not need to make an appointment 'just to talk'. At such times psychotherapists may end up listening to the problem of the person and applying their skills while the person gets what he/she wants however, it is not perceived as a session by a client. Sometimes psychotherapists become flexible in such cases and view this as *pro bono* work.

From above it becomes apparent that flexibility is one of the characteristics a psychotherapist needs in order to be able to provide effective psychotherapy to clients. This sometimes requires amending some aspects of traditional therapy frames.

5.4 Influences of uBuntu on certain practice issues

It is an uBuntu gesture to volunteer and see clients who do not pay, but psychotherapists have bills to pay. As stated in chapter 3, uBuntu is described by using the idiom '*umntu ngumntu ngabantu'* (a human is a human because of other humans) and is characterised by sharing, selflessness, interconnectedness, respect, communalism. In this section I focus on the influences of uBuntu on the setting, gifts and bartering as well as on normalising.

5.4.1 The setting: Taking the service to the people

Traditionally, the therapeutic space includes secluded space, sound proof, enough lighting, and other elements. In traditional African style, people sit around the fire and discuss their personal matters. P6 also reported

> *... we realise that sitting in our offices, people are out there and they need our services, we are failing them ... there is a lot that is happening outside there and it needs our intervention and for us to sit in our offices, I do not think we are helping...*

In an uBuntu setting, a practitioner may consider taking the service to the people. For example, P4 also has taken the service to the people:

> *yes I have done that but not as often, as I say in 12 years those are the 3 consultations.*

This indicates that it is still unusual and not always practical to take the service to the people or to see clients out of the traditional therapy space. In this regard, P2 reflecting on her space for seeing clients said:

> *... mostly in my office, it's not an issue for me as long as it's a secluded area and my client feels safe, my client feels comfortable that they do not have to look around and be worried about who sees me ...*

This emphasises safety and comfort, but also that there is possibly a stigma attached to people attending psychotherapy. The therapy room aassures the privacy of the client and assists in keeping the material confidential.

P7 reported his experiences regarding spaces for psychotherapy and suggests that moving practice from the therapy room outwards may convey important messages to a client.

> *... in my practice life, psychotherapy is not there in the room ...how does that child feel when a psychologist gets into her house? He/she feels valuable, worthy that the*

psychologist here at home it makes something to that client of mine being visited by this person and to me it forms part of psychotherapy that you know.

The above quote also indicates taking the service to the people. Since psychotherapy is about the healing, this can take place in a different space prompted by something else such as a child seeing a psychotherapist getting into his or home. In relation to hospital visits, P3 said:

It's not different, what is important is that privacy, for example when I go there then I would draw/close the curtain and then keep the volume down and talk...

P3 and P8 view hospital rooms as possibilities for conducting psychotherapy. This therefore means that they also consider that clients can be seen out of the traditional therapy space. Participants do not necessarily worry about the issues of space sometimes as P4 reported:

...so they don't feel they have to come to your office to talk about things they feel they can talk to you anywhere.

However, the use of a space for psychotherapy outside the traditional therapy rooms are not without flaws. P8 shared her lived experience:

The sort of challenge is people talking outside, you know they've drawn their curtains and eyes cannot see it but the ears, they will be going about their daily routines. Therefore in any case when people are laying in hospital, they are ill physically so there aren't secrets deep that they want to talk about concerns illness and sometimes certain things about their families, you know, that worry them that they might like, those are the sorts of challenges that happen in my case ...

This means although psychotherapy in other spaces such as hospitals can take place, privacy and confidentiality may be compromised.

Another aspect of uBuntu activities is giving and receiving of gifts as well as exchanging goods for services.

5.4.2 Gifts and bartering

In our amaXhosa tradition when you visit a king (Inkosi) '*uchamel'inkundla*' (you bring a gift). Moreover, if umXhosa gives you a gift and you do not accept it, it is interpreted as you rejecting the owner of the gift. Most psychotherapists are thus faced with a dilemma where we were trained not to accept gifts from clients. Moreover, the ethical code of psychology from HPCSA forbids practitioners to receive gifts from clients. P7 gave an example:

> *It was a cake from one of my clients when I was an intern, I ate it.*

P4 reported:

> *... I once got a slab of chocolate and I took it, it was an oldish age mama of a child and I sort of had this feeling that I cannot take it but I took it, it stayed in my drawer for many years eventually I gave it away to the girls,*

Participant 4 reflected on the gift that was in her disposal for many years that she could not use. Eventually due to discomfort, she gave it away. This means although the participant felt she could not refuse from the client she could not consume it herself because she is aware of the ethics governing her practise, prohibiting practitioners from receiving gifts from clients.

It seems common to most participants have experiences of being offered gifts by clients. P5 also reported:

> *I did have someone who gave me a book but I never opened that book; it's even more than 5 years now. I explained to him: you know we are not encouraged to take stuff from clients and he just insisted that I need to read that book.*

It is interesting to find that although psychotherapists accepted gifts from clients, most of them could not consume those gifts. This means that due to the dilemmas participants are faced with about receiving gifts from clients, dissonance occurs. Psychotherapists feel the need to explain what they did with the gift they received. Receiving a gift from the client and using it seem to be two different processes for participants. P7 reported:

> *Yes it is there on ... of all code of ethics, it is there. It talks about it in ... but don't you think it is going to create harm if I don't accept it? If this person is the only thing she has to show appreciation to me and I say no, what is that going to do to my client if I don't especially if the person was dealing with a rejection, I reject him now to me depends... but it is good to disclose it, it is good to disclose it that is why I disclosed it but I never said I am not going to take it I took it in fact in the whole department we ate that cake.*

Using one's discretion in dealing with some ethical issues is thus the way participants proceeded. Psychotherapists recommend that one way of managing such dilemmas was to disclose the gift to colleagues and even sharing it with them.

In order to justify clients' giving, P7 indicated:

> *To pay for the session and during the internship times you don't have to pay the full money just and that little bit is too much so for her to show appreciation and for me not to break that trust that we have developed for in many sessions knowingly ... I would accept it of course they will not like it.*

In South African institutions where psychologists are trained, psychological services are offered to the public by an intern-psychologist that works under supervision. In such cases the public pays minimum amounts for consultation. Regarding the quotation above, for someone not to afford that minimum amount is indicative of a gross financial constraint. In the above quote, again a practitioner is justifying his reasons for accepting the gift but also indicated that '*they will not like it'*. The 'they' referred to is the qualified psychologists who understand and enforce ethics because they are also in the business of training other psychologists.

Another lived experience involved bartering with clients as an ethical dilemma. P7 indicated the following justifying reasons for bartering:

> *She didn't have money to pay, she didn't have money to pay and the only thing she could give it to me, the only thing that she had was cake. It depends on how to interpret that cake and my interpretation at that time was to say I don't have money to give it to you. This is my appreciation. And bartering was good...*

P7 indicated that although he was scolded by his peers for accepting a cake from a client and had disclosed the gift to the entire psychology department, almost everyone in the department ate/enjoyed the cake. Recommendations on how to deal with this gifts dilemma was made by some participants. P7 shared:

> *That can be helpful to a client but is not actually clearly in our ethics. Why we can't have bartering if it is the only form of payment. If this person has a jersey beautiful jersey that the client has but doesn't have money and this client says this is the only*

this thing that I have for you to show appreciation, would I say no? What do you want me to say do you want me to say no no no please, it depends to what was the presenting and I always like to use an example when I talk about this, of rejection will I be reinforcing rejection if I would say no?

This further illustrates the various considerations that a practitioner would grapple with. Participants are thus frustrated by the confusion felt when faced with receiving gifts and acting 'professionally'. P3 reported, trying to justify her reasons for taking a gift from a client:

> *'Kaloku mna' I'm an African Lumka. And we were no longer now in therapy, we are no longer in that relationship, we have even finished our sessions, you know and now I stood there thinking, oh my God, do I take this fish or not take it. Oh I am going to hurt the feelings of that mom because she's doing it with her heart you know. And I was in a dilemma but I took it, I thought the reason for taking it was this person is giving this with her heart and does not know anything about therapist whatever client relationship and we are not even having those sessions. And I last saw her on my last session. Here now I am saying, no I can't take it. For me it did not feel right and I did not think it was right. So I took the fish, you see, I took the fish because. So now the Western rules would say nope. I mean the client-therapist relationship but as Africans how do you. You know some things as Africans how do you really, hayi maan they are... bayasisokolisa maan* (they make things difficult for us).

The above quotation highlights frustration that is sometimes felt by practitioners when they refer to ethics and the practitioner's traditional background and the confusion these cause. Authorities who see to the adherence of ethics are blamed for making things difficult for practitioners by not understanding their dilemma caused by such experiences.

The above quotes human-ness and empathy for the client. It seems as though participants recommend giving and receiving gifts to and from clients in a responsible manner that does not exploit any of the two parties.

5.4.3 Normalising

To normalise is to change something in order to fit the standard norm. For example the idiom '*akuhlanga lungehlanga'* is translated as what has happened to you has happened before. This is an amaXhosa way of normalising difficult experience that is painful to deal with. In this occurrence P5 normalises by externalising, she reports:

> *...especially with couples I like to externalise issues like you guys are fine but there's a problem with the relationship, let's look at the relationship, so that they can remain at least know that there are ok but the issue is with the relationship and see how the interactions in the relationship is affecting them . So I like to do that with couples...*

Again, P5 expressed her way of normalising by reporting:

> *I normalise with people who are traumatised to say you know what you are going through it's normal, it's normal for a person who has been through trauma, for instance when the person is avoiding, to avoid going to that space or sometimes is avoiding even to think about it and even to talk about it.*

In both quotations above, P5 seems to be normalising within the boundaries of acceptable practice in psychotherapy. On the other hand P6 reported:

> *I share my personal experiences to a limited extent... at the same time people come to me not to hear about me, they come to me for my professional services, so I do not want it to turn out to be about me as if I am anybody on the street, but if I feel that it is relevant, I will.*

The above examples show that there is professional practice expected from psychotherapists to normalise. One of the golden rules of ethics is 'do no harm', which a therapist must be cognisant of every time therapy frames are at play. In other words it is recommended by participants that one must always be cognisant of beneficence.

5.5 Suggestions for psychotherapy expansions

Psychotherapy is a formally structured intervention. It is therefore apparent that it must have rules and guidelines. The diagram below illutrates some suggestions fro expanding psychotherapy.

Figure 5.3: Suggestions for psychotherapy expansions

A subtheme on suggestions of psychotherapy expansions was the split between the Eurocentric way of doing psychotherapy and the reality psychotherapists are faced when practising psychotherapy on amaXhosa clients.

5.5.1 Western-reality dichotomy

Psychotherapy is a foreign concept to amaXhosa and is fairly new. amaXhosa were using and are still using other methods of healing such as traditional healers or diviners. P8 shared:

> *...and people had no belief in it* [meaning psychotherapy], *they expected serious reservation it could ever work. What is that thing psychologist? When there are traditional healers to deal with that, with certain issues that I will be dealing with, but I wanted to give it a try and give the people a try or exposure to psychology.*

amaXhosa Psychologists are faced with the dissonance of acting in their tradition or according to their training when dealing with amaXhosa clients. After she was asked a question of whether she would hug a client again, P2 responded:

> *... I would with so much difficulty actually to stop this child not to hug, it would not be easy for me to stop that. ... as much as I'm saying I'm championing boundaries but it's difficult then for me for somebody who's showing uBuntu for somebody who's being grateful who is saying thank you to say to them I will not hug them, I have never said that to anyone that I don't hug.*

Some behaviours or gestures are expected in amaXhosa culture: some amaXhosa do like them but may also do them because they are expected to act in a certain way.

5.5.2 Contrasts to Western training

Psychologists professional training does not distinguish between Africans and Europeans, we all get trained in the same class using the same curriculum. Confusion on what to do for amaXhosa start to take place when in practice. P4 indicated her experience:

> *... to that stage whereby I feel like okay there's a little bit of a blur between me the person and me the therapist, it gets to that level that I am giving my time...I cannot end at this particular point in time, sort of I have to sacrifice my certain time so we can wrap up...*

The participant means although the therapeutic hour has lapsed, there are issues that are not clearly explained to the client then the participant uses her time to explain such issues and termination of the session at the expected time becomes impractical in that sense. This is one of the contrasts between African and Eurocentric way of practice in that in the Western way of practice if the therapeutic hour has ended the session stops but in an African way one says what one came to say until one finishes. Another contrast between Western professional training and practicalities in working with amaXhosa clients include going further to assist than what is expected by Western standards. P3 shared:

> *... But now then it looks like in inverted commas my relationship now is going beyond the four walls that we sit in with the client. Because I think these rules confine us to the four walls, that we do the counselling, you know, in. And also these rules, hey these rules maan, I don't know I think sometimes they just clash with who we are, how do I separate myself, those are my values besides uBuntu I really like, I really like serving people.*

This quote highlights the frustrations of psychotherapist feeling restricted to be themselves in servicing clients. In such cases psychotherapists feel torn between themselves and their profession. P4 shared:

> *... So I think there is a certain level of Cris-cross between the elements of uBuntu and ground rules and the framing of therapy because with uBuntu, this feeling that you have, you feel that you cannot be asking people to observe those rules because it feels*

harsh, it feels impersonal, it feels too formal, so yes that is definitely a Cris-cross, surely it is… I will tell you this, having worked as long as I have, I do not know how things are now in terms of current training programs but our training is Western.

This is another frustrating dilemma that amaXhosa psychotherapists are faced with. Western principles seem to be restricting amaXhosa clients from services their people in the way that works for the profession and for the nature of clientele.

amaXhosa psychotherapists seem to be directing most of their frustration as being caused by the governing body, the HPCSA. P7 said:

… I'm coming from the university where I spent a lot of time speaking English to clients, but this was an old woman I had to speak Xhosa and the challenge was hey how do I take the psychology concept into Xhosa, how do I change that psychological concept if I want to explain something to her in Xhosa which I had to think of my own explanation, you know, … they think I am a fixer. …I wish I can do something but in terms of bus fare ha! we would have a problem me and the HPCSA.

P7 means that other challenges that are posed to African psychotherapists include that psychology is taught in English and he then struggled to explain certain psychological concepts to a client that could not speak English. This then is one dilemma. Another dilemma he is referring to is the expectations of umXhosa client leading to a conscious ignoring of HPCSA rules to assist a fellow human being who needs help such as a bus fare. P7 continues:

It is the same thing uBuntu I was never taught about uBuntu. uBuntu says you must go all out as long that this person is getting what he or she was looking for. I was never taught that what I was taught the frameworks not uBuntu …

This implies that in P7's university curriculum uBuntu was not part of it, although it is a big part of the participant's everyday living. An umXhosa trainee psychologist who practised among umXhosa client was rebuked for practising in an amaXhosa way, as P7 shared. This seems as though amaXhosa practitioners are not understood by the health professions governing body and the frustration levels of amaXhosa are escalating. Clients are being serviced and no harm is done while other methods or ways of practice are not endorsed. P3 explained:

... the client therapy relationship it ends here in the practise. And that's a Western culture really, I don't know, you know these rules some of them are so Western because what's wrong with me if I'm going to pass that way because it's not taking me out of my way, what's wrong with me not taking it and then in the next session give it to him...

P3 means that part of uBuntu is to assist another human being when you can in any way possible, but psychology has discouraged her from doing so with her clients. This poses a dissonance between her way of doing things and her training.

I take it case by case, I mean you just looking at the situation, analysing it, analysing the situation, I'm emphasising that, analysing it and then you sort of like get the wisdom which way to go.

P3 in this case emphasises that she uses her instinct to deal with situations because her university training did not give her proper guidelines on how to deal with those specific situations. This also reflects on some of the dilemmas that are facing amaXhosa psychotherapists

5.5.3 Psychoeducation

I think it is also important to educate on topics that people are not familiar with. Regarding psychoeducation P2 reported:

... I use that first session to just let them know what counselling is all about and what expectations are so that we are able to meet their needs.

P2 incorporates psychoeducation in the introductory session. In this regard P6 shared her ways of working further by saying:

… even within psychotherapy I teach. I also teach them about marriage,... I teach them about life and understanding life.

This example about marriage implies that psychoeducation an important part of psychotherapy. P7 indicated:

... when they come for therapy through the questioning they kind of find out that no I am the one who is supposed to take the ownership of the reason that they are here, and the expectations changes...

This means that psychoeducation is done at the beginning of the psychotherapy relationship and clients are made to realise that they are the ones who will act, become and change according to the goals of psychotherapy.

It seems as though amaXhosa psychotherapists use psychoeducation as a tool in their sessions. This could be due to the fact that most clients' expectations of psychotherapy are reflective of an incorrect understanding of how psychotherapy must be conducted. Psycho-educating therefore may alleviate some of the misconceptions about psychotherapy that exist.

5.5.4 Fear of the law/HPCSA

In many of the examples given, the participants showed that they were fearful of consequences they may be faced with should they not follow the rules of doing psychotherapy participants perceived HPCSA as the law and a body that is there to punish them. P3 illustrated this fear in:

I hope you are not going to contact Health Professions Council and then I'm put under discipline or whatever.

It is obvious that these amaXhosa psychotherapists view HPCSA as an unapproachable authority that fails to understand people but only implement rules and regulations. Psychotherapists are clearly afraid of HPCSA. In this regard P7 indicated:

... during the CPD sessions we don't talk about the economical issues of our clients in the CPD sessions we talk about many other things that are very good as well ... Because people they actually they are blind folded they think that the ethics, yes the ethics are there to guide us, but sometimes other things are not there in the ethics...

Whilst this participant values some of the material presented when attending CPD, he shows frustrations about the lack of application of such material to everyday practise; where some aspects are not clarified.

Some psychotherapeutic approaches do not emphasise considering the influences of the past, but this is important to the meaning-making of amaXhosa. P8 shared:

> *But I suppose you might call it a clash in a sense that in a Western or to a Western mind you would look especially in phenomenological settings you would look at a phenomenon as such and not look or you'd feel discouraged to look in past or draw from any wisdom or theories and look at the thing as is right now and the space and here and now.*

It seems that amaXhosa psychotherapists are faced with clients who have expectations connected to their way of living. Our training as psychotherapists is Western while we are Africans.

5.5.5 Psychotherapy and other systems

Suggestions and experiences of psychotherapists about South African universities and the psychology curriculum are made. Psychologists feel that their training should be designed such that it is relevant to a wider South African community and should prepare students for the real South African life for the majority. P6 reported:

> *… I do not know who develops curriculum for psychologists ... make it relevant to people and to the needs of society because we need to have lots of psychologists outside and inside. ... for example ... he is doing psychotherapy in his kombi and he goes to the community and see people in that kombi. That's how we should think. Sitting as we are sitting in the office not the same, in fact number 1 is it is accessible to the chosen few and few people can afford, these people out there do not have medical aid and we have to reach those people ... [in class] there will be two Xhosa speakers and 8 English speakers, so it is not user friendly, ... so they must take more Blacks so they are able to see a broader community.*

During training, more emphasis should be put on the practicalities of applying psychotherapy skills to people. P7 noted that the teaching about ethical codes was more theoretical, before people had practice experience, so this led to anxieties about applications:

> *... when you are studying you are actually making sure that you comply with HPCSA as well as the academic department, and you don't do much practicals, you are not trained to deal with practical issues in the department other than to understand*

policies, the code of ethics and how to actually implement modalities. But when I started my private practice ... I was anxious...

However, P4 was supportive of the need for ethical guidelines and boundaries recognising the risks of not having such knowledge:

> *...because our work involves so much emotions it is sometimes easy for boundaries to blur and I sort of always feel that you need to establish so that by the time the process moves along and gets intense at least at the back of one's mind... I am aware that there are rules that we still need to observe... because therapy is a formally structured scene so they (boundaries) are important, it does not always mean that they are actually always observed.*

Again above, the participant notes that abstract guidelines might not always be applied. Her words above and below show that she emphasises her values and the need for warmth in relating. In addition, she appears to be more confident with her style of practice: P3 reported:

> *...how do I separate ... who I am, the values I live my life... by with these therapeutic thingies, it's part of who I am... that's also the environment I am in of uBuntu. You know not being cold, having that cold relationship ... and I don't feel guilty about anything, I mean I have helped my fellow human being and I would do it even if I was not counselling that person...*

In summary, participants made suggestions of being culturally sensitive in universities when training psychotherapists and creating training programmes that will emphasise more practical work and less emphasis on the rules of ethical codes and boundaries. Participants suggested that psychology curriculum in all South African universities could better integrate culture-sensitive diversity and ethics. amaXhosa psychotherapists feel excluded in the curriculum and practice of psychotherapy and this exclusion brings about dissonance to them as practitioners. Participants emphasised that although they may divert guidelines in order to bring good service and healing to their African clients, they were cognisant of the non-maleficence principle. This do no harm principle was perceived as guiding participants towards making sound decisions in certain situations.

5.5 Focus group

Formatting of the focus group is discussed in this section. The purpose of this focus group was to discuss my synthesis of the findings of the individual interviews with participants so that they assist in checking my 'blind spots' as a researcher and add information that could be left out. The findings that were presented to my participants appear in appendix E; the following additional information was provided.

5.6.1 Socialisation factors

Participants concurred with the findings and no new information was added except for giving more examples of these socialisation factors. They concurred with the language issues that were raised that language is important in psychotherapy sessions for communication purposes. Regarding gender issues participants agreed that the amaXhosa nation is predominantly patriarchal. The understanding of amaXhosa traditions is important to understand the way of living of amaXhosa. The Eastern Cape Province context influences the socio-economic status of people living in it.

5.6.2 Adherence to psychotherapy principles

Participants felt that university training is culture biased, where African culturally influenced ways of living are not included. Participants made mention of the use e-counselling and of social media as a new and becoming popular way for making appointments and booking for sessions. They were excited about including e-counselling in their scope of practice but were concerned about confidentiality and privacy issues which may be compromised by the use of technology. Participants indicated that even though they keep things confidential and private between themselves and clients, clients sometimes do not adhere to such ethical values in that they sometimes discuss their problems or give feedback in public spaces. This becomes uncomfortable to participants but they seem not to be able to control it successfully.

5.6.3 Therapy frames and adjustments

Participants indicated that they felt uncomfortable when they had to deal with issues that are culturally acceptable but discouraged by the Eurocentric styles of practice. In terms of accepting gifts from clients they indicated that there will always be a danger such as the client may need favours later on, although not to accept it may be perceived as rejection by the client.

Another new added point was the issue of referring clients to other healers such as prophets or *izangoma*: participants felt that it was outside of their scope of practices. They indicated that it was not controlled. Spiritual issues came out as issues that always arise in practice. This indicated one of the dilemmas experienced by amaXhosa psychotherapists sometimes where they are torn between spiritual issues; which are one of the core living ways of amaXhosa and psychotherapy practice; which does not encourage dealing with spiritual issues.

In terms of African time participants indicated that they call clients to remind them of their sessions and if they still do not show, then they will charge for sessions that were not cancelled within 24 hours, but they would feel guilty about charging. They indicated that their feeling guilty about charging for no show sessions was related to uBuntu.

5.6.4 Influences of uBuntu on certain practice issues

In terms of the setting participants indicated that they were mostly willing to conduct sessions anywhere convenient however they were most comfortable conducting sessions in their psychotherapy rooms. They gave examples of sessions that were conducted in hospitals, coffee shops, in the homes of clients where there were disturbances that they were not able to control; which impacted negatively on those sessions.

In terms of normalising, participants shared that they used personal as well as other people's experiences that were similar to those of their clients as examples to normalise situations their clients were faced with.

For gifts and bartering participants indicated that they had challenges because even though they included in their introductory sessions that they cannot receive gifts from the clients; clients still left gifts with their receptionists or insisted that they take the gifts. Participants were torn between taking their training and their cultural practises in that not taking a gift implied rejecting a client and receiving it implied that they were going against their professional training as psychotherapists.

Participants added and highlighted differences between ways of living that are Western influenced and African influenced. For example what is culturally applauded and appreciated in African attitudes, like a person that decides to look after his family and stay in his family home, whereas in the Western perspective that can be perceived a lack of personal development or dependency syndrome. A person is accompanied when going to see a doctor, so this may be why people attend psychological sessions accompanied by a friend or a relative.

On the point that uBuntu is not without faults, participants indicated that some of the disadvantages of uBuntu that were highlighted included that African people feel obligated to help even if the help sometimes is disadvantageous for the one being helped. Another point raised was that family members become demanding and feel entitled to benefit from the achievements of the family member that seems to have more resources that they do. In relation to cultural changes, P5 shared

> *I am trying to explain this thing context ... sometimes in nowadays it will be misinterpreted you know and greeting people is also part of uBuntu ya those things and going out of the way to help another person its quite complex really there's various issues or facets to it. Yes sometime if even winding down your window to give something to someone on the road you think twice nowadays that's why I'm saying its context dependent as well.*

To conclude, suggestion on how to define uBuntu were made such and it was emphasised that uBuntu definition should include such cultural practices that prioritises the value of the people humanity, kindness, that African people do not align themselves with tacit nature in that they are not always aware of the knowledge they possess or how I can be valuable to others.

PART B: uBuntu

This section focuses on uBuntu and responds to research questions 2, 3 and 4, namely:

- What uBuntu principles are applicable to psychotherapy practice experienced by psychotherapists?
- What are the experiences of psychotherapists (positive and negative) regarding incorporating uBuntu into their practice?
- What can the study recommend in relation to incorporating uBuntu into psychotherapy?

I start by giving the definitions of uBuntu according to understandings of participants, then go on to define uBuntu as an African way of living, and discuss the faults of uBuntu as described. Thereafter I share experiences of psychotherapists about uBuntu principles that are applicable to psychotherapy and I finalise this section by discussing uBuntu misrepresentations.

5.7 Defining uBuntu

Participants were asked to give their own definitions of uBuntu in the interviews. P2 defined uBuntu as:

> *uBuntu comes from the word 'umntu'* (human), *so uBuntu is being human, it's being humane, its loving others unconditionally, maybe, I can't be love because I'm not God but it's giving love to others it's being compassionate, it's giving the little that you have, the ability to share with others, and not necessarily monetarily... lending an ear if somebody's asking for directions taking a few seconds out of your time and say look that is the route that you must take. That's uBuntu sharing something of your own to others. I try at all times to give of what I know of the knowledge that I have, to disseminate the skills that I think you need so I would say you probably need this, have you tried that? That's uBuntu, sharing of whatever I know...*

P2's understanding of uBuntu thus highlights unconditional love, compassion, giving and sharing, helping, giving your time or knowledge, skill, and assisting people including strangers. P3 expands on the human-ness of uBuntu as indicated:

uBuntu is about humanity, humanity, helping others and not help only your own, the fact that that person is a human being you extend a hand of help and also being generous, ... for example as Africans you know the extended family thing you help the relatives, you don't only help the immediate ones. When you educate, you also educate relatives you pay for their education and all. I mean even people you do not know, you would, some people in our culture they will take them and stay with them and help them ...this is a human being let me just treat that person with respect and also take care of my fellow human being in whatever way, it does not have to be money, in whatever way.

This illustrates an emphasis on generosity that goes beyond the immediate family. P8 shared his perception of uBuntu by also emphasising human solidarity:

uBuntu to me now means human humanity, humanness to be a human being any other being.

In uBuntu traditional settings relationships are important. Trust is one of the important features of a good relationship. This good relationship and trust becomes the basis for interdependence of people to one another. P4 indicated:

... people will knock on your door and request a cup of sugar without feeling anxious that you are going to get it, ... that kind of knowing that you can absolutely rely on someone without thinking too much about it, that is important, and that there is an understanding between these two people that you can rely on each other ... it is automatic. ...it's feeling of knowing deeply deep down knowing that no matter what you do there is someone who is available and willing to provide that kind of a feeling.

P4 thus emphasises being able to rely on each other leading to a deeper sense of being supported.

The following quote responds to research question one; what uBuntu principles are applicable to psychotherapy practice experienced by psychotherapists? Participants felt that the profession requires them to behave in a way that does not suit their way of living following uBuntu. P1 indicated:

It is in me, ikum kaloku endidalwe nayo and ndiyayazba kaloku (it is in me, it is something I was born with) *and I know when to give someone a break it is something that we have to do and I know at the back of my mind that we are not allowed to do this.*

This refers to help whether permanent or temporal as a principle of uBuntu. It means a brief provision of basic needs to someone that offers a breather while the person is busy figuring out what to do about their unfortunate situation such as poverty. This highlights another dissonance and some tensions experienced by participants between cultural values and professional structures. This contradicts the Eurocentric psychotherapy that implies that psychotherapy helps one to help himself.

5.7.1 uBuntu defined as an African way of life

This section responds to research question 3: what are the experiences of psychotherapists (positive and negative) regarding incorporating uBuntu into their practice?
uBuntu is a value that is so embedded in the African way of life; it is often confused with other personal characteristics and values. P3 noted in this regard:

I do not know whether it is uBuntu or it is a gift I have of having mercy or I am a person who is very nurturing...

Thus P3 emphasises associated personal qualities for P6 uBuntu includes, empathy, caring and putting other people before self, she indicated:

My understanding of uBuntu it encompasses understanding of another person's situations some form of empathy, sort of. And also like caring for the other person and having that understanding that with other problems you have to put another person first

These features indicated by P6 seem to be related to a way of living of African people; whilst they can be features of most human beings, the element of putting others before self is emphasised more. Another example of a definition of uBuntu as a way of living of African people is indicted by P7 as:

Bishop Tutu's term 'you made me to be who I am'. Being responsible for one another, accounting to one another, being ethical and morally upright to one another to me would be equal to uBuntu.

This definition involves moral standards that include an element of accountability to others, which is embedded in the premise humans are humans through other humans.

P7 also expands on its qualities that span all aspects of life, no matter what the context. P7 expands these defining characteristics of uBuntu by giving examples such as the use of personal resources such as money and home, investing in the futures of others, care, sharing and respect. This illustrates that uBuntu reaches all aspects of interactions.

... uBuntu is a life style, it is what you are supposed to do not outside the therapy room even inside the therapy room that is a life style... In fact without uBuntu in all the frameworks, your framework is not going to work in our culture ... Person Centred Therapy that is first one that I was taught, huh do you think it is going to work hey in my culture ...where you being non-judgmental, be there for your client, be congruent and all of that, yes but without doing it (uBuntu) *to your client it is not going to work... let me practice it and not be judgmental... it is much more practical you know it puts meat in the skeleton for me in any framework that I was taught ...hey if there is no uBuntu in all of those I have mentioned there is no practice there it is not going to work for me.*

P7 further highlights that for amaXhosa uBuntu is a way of living therefore it is beneficial in addition to the psychotherapy process to include uBuntu in a style of practice of any psychotherapist treating amaXhosa clients regardless of the modality. Furthermore, P7 also accentuates another dilemma faced by psychotherapists where theory in class does not correspond to the actual practice, so there is the need for practical examples of what a practitioner will come across. P7's lived experiences then are concretising theory, putting meat on the skeleton, so to speak.

P5 shared her understanding of uBuntu as context and era dependant. Her understanding of uBuntu also involves sharing and caring, reaching out to strangers:

I think it's also context dependent coz I remember when I was growing up you'll see someone passing by and someone would say hey where are you going and she say I'm going to such a place "no come here man and get some Marhewu (drink) that place is far" and if maybe is towards dusk the person can be invited to come in and proceed with the journey the next day.

Although practising uBuntu may be taking more from the person who is practising it, people that are socialised in uBuntu are willing to keep on practising it. In this instance P7 indicated:

...and the challenge is ... I need to pay for this space that I am in and that's a challenge and to pay these people that are working here if I do voluntarily work, so it's actually compromising my pocket for the office, but well I take from my salary where I work as long as I felt good about what I was doing.

P7 continued by including an element of compromise in his understanding of uBuntu:

It makes me feel good because it is the right thing to do to see that the other person is actually assisted even if you don't gain anything from it even if it is compromising your own personal life...

Thus P5 and P7 both define uBuntu by including going out of one's way to help a fellow human being. The above are indicative of uBuntu experiences that participants shared.

uBuntu is not without flaws. Some people take advantage of others in the name of uBuntu. P5 reported:

... I have to take him home, you know things like that and I just say that I didn't know about that. That I'm not taking you home. I actually took that client home (laughs) you know it as part of uBuntu but... sometimes I say bloody Black people because the mother drove him and she didn't say anything to me I discovered that from the client.

Sometimes people take others for granted in the name of uBuntu. It happens that after going out of one's way to assist someone, the least one expects is appreciation from the person on the receiving end. P7 however noted:

Some appreciate, some do not ...

This means that some clients do not appreciate his/her going out of the way to assist them. It is expected of a fellow Black human being to help. The dilemmas experienced by participants in the above section are caused by the fact that they are trying to comply with the principles of psychotherapy of the west while treating amaXhosa.

To summarise then, common characteristics or values of uBuntu that seem to define or describe uBuntu are as follows: human-ness, sharing, trust, interdependence, being, non-judgmental, care, selflessness, loving unconditionally, responsible for one another.

5.7.2 Principles of uBuntu

This section responds to research question 2; What uBuntu principles are applicable to psychotherapy practice experienced by psychotherapists?

5.7.2.1 Interdependence / interconnectedness

In amaXhosa culture, people do not share their experiences or challenges outside of their clan or a senior person in their village, be it *Inkosi* (king), *usibonda* (community leader) *umfundisi* (reverend) or others. Such leaders are not trained in those leadership positions; rather they are seen to be elected by ancestors or God. A psychotherapist on the other hand is formally trained to hold the position of being an "advisor" as the elected do. To gain credibility from an individual client and for this umXhosa client to be able to share his/her problems with the psychotherapist they have to connect with the psychotherapist somehow. Participants reported their lived experiences. For example P4 said:

> *... the fact that our culture is like that, we have that connection...you are someone comfortable they want to talk to...*

While P2 reported:

> *I am Black because you are Black, maybe I'm the last person who know who could salvage them so I would kinda help them, I will try hard to help them where I can.*

P2 shared another way of encouraging interdependence:

> *Almost tell them how to buddy, you know at the beginning of the year you are always trained how to buddy students who can buddy others.*

In isiXhosa any woman who is in the age of your mother is your mother, she has the right to reprimand you when you did something that was unacceptable, or commend you if you did something that your mother would be proud of. P2 indicated:

I think that being an adult, being a parent, being Black sitting with a Black student [as a client] *I know what their mother would say to them or their aunt would say to them, I would also risk being that mother...*

A psychotherapist refers to a client as a relative, even though the client is not a blood relative, but because they come from a similar background they are interconnected. P7 indicated:

I think I did what I was supposed to do for my brother.

In this excerpt P7 refers to a client as a brother. As indicated earlier these uBuntu principles are intertwined, for example interconnections, also bring about help, compassion and sharing.

Ploughing back to one's community after one had succeeded in her studies or business is a gesture that is expected in an uBuntu way of living. Nowadays this ploughing back to your community or family is often called 'Black Tax'. However, successful people who do not contribute are perceived as aloof and disconnected to their community members. By displaying signs of togetherness with people in one's community one indicates still being interconnected. In this instance P7 added:

You know I even now, I do ...voluntarily work at the same time in my practice in the spirit of uBuntu. I see that as ploughing back without any monetary things.

P7 also reported the need at times to make home visits, even though this was sanctioned in training:

Let me get another example of uBuntu you know at the university I was never taught to say as a psychologist you can actually visit a client, go and visit a client where the client stays, they said that is the work of social workers no not you as a psychologist don't do that okay I work with NGOs. I work with NGOs I go to the NGO, I visit the orphans the same clients coming to me I visit them and I found out the more I get in touch with their households and I get to be known by the families the better the therapy will be...

Again, this displays the principle of help, sharing and love which are also part of interconnections between humans.

5.7.2.2 Respect

Respect (*ukuhlonipha*) is one the overlapping principles between the Western, amaXhosa and uBuntu ways of doing things. Emphasising the importance of respect in psychotherapy, P7 reported:

> *… I am a Xhosa and as a Xhosa I expect that I should be respectful to older people…*

This means that displaying respect when dealing with older clients creates good interrelations, helping to reassure an older person to be able to open up so she can obtain the assistance she came to receive. This is very important to amaXhosa. In some instances an elderly person will refer to the younger person showing respect by saying '*unobuntu ke lo mntwana'*,(this child has humanity) implying this is a good, well behaved young person.

Respecting the people's beliefs is part of respecting them as humans. In this regard P3 indicated:

> *…Xhosa rituals and all that, I use that for them to be healed, for example they believe that a person is not dead, is there, not dead, so the technique that I would use is to for example, ok go to the grave yard and speak your heart to that person and say whatever depending on what we were talking about and all that, and they would go and say ... well that person is dead is not there but this is symbolic.*

The above example illustrates ways of utilising aspects of the belief system about ancestors as part of the therapeutic process. Building on the respect for a person's beliefs, P2 indicated the importance of respect for one another even when not sharing the same beliefs.

> *... even if I am Black I may not believe in some of the practises African people practise. But out of respect,…whatever is happening in their life, I'll be respectful of that so there's no conflicting…, it is not something I have never heard of, it is not shocking news, when I hear of it so I am able to listen to what they are saying and be respectful.*

People are respected for their belief systems and this has implications for the ways in which one shows care for others through actions. P3 continued:

> *Just that this is a human being let me just treat that person with respect and also take care of my fellow human being in whatever way; it does not have to be money, in whatever way.*

P2 shares the same sentiments about respecting people:

> *... so I am able to listen to what they are saying and be respectful.*

This means that respecting another human being may be shown in different ways. Listening to and taking care of a person can be a ways of displaying respect, reflecting uBuntu principles.

5.7.2.3 Going the extra mile

It is within uBuntu practice to put others before you. Part of uBuntu practice is to go out of your way to assist a fellow human being in a spirit of solidarity. P3 reported:

> *I always go an extra mile, and I found that I will be doing it in my practise things that this person is supposed to be doing, I will be doing... I am doing things that I'm not supposed to be doing, they must be doing them themselves.*

This means although participant does not have a professional obligation to assist clients by doing additional paperwork or negotiations with other agencies (things the client 'is supposed' to do) for them; this illustrates understanding the predicament clients may find themselves in due to various factors such as affordability and lack of resources. In uBuntu this is an acceptable practise, seen as a participant sharing resources.

Going beyond what is professionally expected is also noted by P4 who indicated:

> *… I do feel like I am going a little bit beyond but it is formally expected...I am stepping a little bit beyond what I am expected to*

This participant is cognisant of her role as a psychotherapist, but that does not stop her from practicing in a way that from other perspectives could be regarded as interfering with the client's autonomy.

In a case where a client was to be unfairly judged in a court of law, a participant who understood the conditions that led to the behaviour went an extra mile to ensure that the client received help instead of punishment. Referring to the case P4 added:

> *... I found myself working so hard that people could understand how much his environment, his upbringing, his family situation could have contributed...*

This means the participant went beyond what was expected of her for the benefit of the client. Highlighting her assisting beyond her professional role, P1 gives the following example:

> *I went to the social workers and asked for food parcels for her. ...You see I went out of the office and helped her look for food, I became a social worker...*

In isiXhosa tradition it is the younger person that goes to the older one when there is something that needs to be discussed. It is the older person that has the right to say '*yiz'apha*' (come here). P7 says in such cases obtains permission from guardians to assist a younger person by visiting their homes. This reflects a psychotherapist going an extra-mile to assist a client.

> *The old mamas the old tatas can't come to my place and sometimes I need to ask something from them and I know they can't come here and these NGOs will tell me the address and I will go there through the permission of my client you know.*

In this case the psychotherapist could chose to obtain collateral information telephonically or otherwise but P7 chose to go an extra-mile.

As indicated by participants in this section, participants do different things that indicate that they go an extra-mile for their clients. This seems to be influenced by their compassion, which is also one of the elements of uBuntu.

5.7.2.4 Spirituality

Spirituality forms a greater part of uBuntu, where people feel the interconnectedness through seen and unseen spirits. In this regard P6 reported:

> *when we move to spirituality, then I can share something. ... as I am working and also growing and also developing myself and on the other side realised that spirituality helps a lot...we need to look at people in totality. ...I will not like my client not to tap into spirituality because I believe it is the most important thing.*

This means the participant incorporates spirituality in her sessions in order to provide a comprehensive and inclusive service to clients, understanding that it is inevitable not to ignore spirituality when dealing with people who have uBuntu as the way of living.

Spirituality can be in different forms, for example within the amaXhosa, some people believe in ancestors that manifest themselves physically as snakes called '*umajola'*. When the '*umajola'* appears the belief is that there is interconnectedness between the person and his/her ancestors. Others believe in, '*uQamata' 'uThixo wamanyange'* (God of ancestors), while others have faith in Jesus Christ, sometimes called '*uThixo wabelungu'* (God of white people). It would appear that psychotherapists also are aware of their own belief systems and would follow one of the above traditions, or another. This is a sensitive topic among amaXhosa families. P1 illustrates how having a similar background enhances understanding:

> *... culturally I understand them, when they talk about issues that are happening at home, like amasiko* (traditional ceremonies) *and all that. Sometimes those issues come in this practice and I am able to actually listen to those and understand them better.*

Whilst P1 might not feel comfortable engaging clients much on spiritual issues, she does not prevent clients from sharing their beliefs.

As noted earlier, P3 also indicated that she uses a metaphor of encouraging clients who believe that talking to a grave may bring some kind of a relief in what they are experiencing. She says:

> *... they believe that a person is not dead.... go to the grave yard and speak your heart to that person*

This participant indicated that she uses this technique in context. Whilst in the past psychology has been discouraging of psychotherapists from dealing with spiritual issues in sessions, in our contexts it may be expected of psychologists to refer clients to *izangoma's*, or diviners should spiritual issues be foregrounded by clients. This may be the reason for most of my participants to be reluctant to share more about their use of spirituality in sessions because there is some sensitivity about being judged from a more medical perspective.

5.7.2.5 Sharing, caring, humility, selfless-ness

Acting in an uBuntu way involves providing services for people without charging for those services. In other words, practitioners may at times share their psychotherapeutic skills and time with others at no charge as an act of uBuntu. P6 reported:

... the fact that I am doing this community services for those around, young wives it shows uBuntu and I have cared for them, in my therapy I can say even the fact that ... after the termination I still communicate with that person...

The above participant therefore alludes to continued contact after termination of psychotherapy, which could be questioned. Regarding sharing resources that may be useful to a fellow human being as an act of uBuntu, P5 said:

...giving someone a book that you think it might help its part of sharing; like I did have a client who came to me because she was recently diagnosed of HIV so I do have area of interest I do have lot of literature hands out this and that I share see if there's anything we can talk about it.

Such practice might be acceptable practice in certain forms of psychotherapy, but here the participant constructs this as a part of sharing, a characteristic of uBuntu. The above examples by P5 and P6 are contributions in other people's lives as a sign that they care for other people. It is a quality of uBuntu to care and to keep connections with other people, as displayed in the above quotes.

P6 also emphasises the caring that is stated above by saying:

There is no way that you would be in a health profession and not practice uBuntu, because we are dealing with people... the mere fact that you are dealing with people must include certain aspects of uBuntu. ... we are human beings, when you are dealing with human issues there is no way you can divorce yourself, I am not saying you must also share yours but how can you understand that person's problem if you are inhuman, how can you?

Here P6 shows an awareness of the boundaries of not sharing one's own problems with clients, but also reiterates the shared humanity of the work, also emphasised by uBuntu.

P4 adds to the above by noting the satisfaction when getting a positive responses after displaying uBuntu practice:

I think cases like that are cases that make you realise how meaningful your work can be, without being big headed about it but really it cuts to the core of what humanity is… being humane, yes it is how important it could be in someone's life, actually saving someone's life.

This means the participant feels encouraged by the output of her work. It seems that the incorporation of uBuntu in practice impacts positively on both clients and psychotherapists.

The use of uBuntu in psychotherapy enables psychotherapists to be viewed as humans by clients, rather than this omniscient kind of creature. As a psychologist that is practising from home regarding one of her humble behaviours, P5 reported:

I do that sometimes and sometimes I do accompany my clients on foot just instead of leaving them at the gate if I don't have another client I just walk down with them I do that sometimes I just walk down with them.

The above example of walking along beside a client may be viewed by some perspectives as somewhat intrusive or undermining the client's privacy; however she seems to give this example to illustrate reassurance or that she too is willing to walk along. Some gestures displayed by participants from the goodness of their hearts are translated into uBuntu practises. In the context where very often grandparents carry additional responsibilities for children, care might be demonstrated by making an effort beyond what is expected.

P4 reported:

… I will pick up a phone and call the parent, but usually the grandmothers, with grannies in particular I always feel like I do need to go a step further in what I do…

The above example shows the practitioner's desire to promote interconnections. A further example of this is from P2 who gave the example of:

… students coming from other African countries that had an accent that was difficult to hear, I'll take them again because I think I have some compassion in me, I did feel for them through I realise that we were struggling.

This means not giving up on them because the psychotherapist finds difficulty due to accent challenges but to work with the person until the problem is managed. In other words this illustrates being selfless, as uBuntu would encourage.

Traditionally, psychotherapists see clients by appointment only, but this might not always be the case as P2 indicated:

> *… I did not see clients who had appointments only,... sometimes it does not mean that I am not busy but I make time to see that client...that is uBuntu. That giving of some of my time...*

To see clients without arranging proper appointments is a sign of uBuntu. In addition, it might be perceived as rude to be too goal-directed, so the practitioner shows patience with a client, in order that the person feels heard. The guidelines of psychology indicate that for privacy purposes practitioners could not relate to clients in public; but that in more traditional settings, such boundaries might be perceived as being uncaring; and this places amaXhosa practitioners in potentially awkward situations because they understand their cultural traditions and their training. In this regard P3 reported:

> *There are cases whereby I see that ya as Africans whereby ok this one, no I must draw a line. For example you'll get a person you've been in therapy with and then when that person sees you in Shoprite or in whatever shop. ... you try in a nice polite way of not respond and try to steer this person and talk about something else you see.*

In amaXhosa traditions, adults have the right to say whatever they to people younger than him. Children do not have the right to express their feelings to adults. However, in contrast to this psychotherapy meets clients at the point of need regardless of their age. P2 reported:

> *I was the adult in the counselling session, ...uBuntu you allow them to ventilate and say whatever they wish to say, when they were younger, you know as an adult you could easily say or willed your power or authority... uBuntu for me sometimes is just going to their level not seeing myself as this person who is in power and authority. But uBuntu is becoming the mother sometimes I could actually feel sometimes now this is not the professional speaking, I think I am going beyond that because I'm also a mother so I could tell sometimes when it's not on psychology speaking but I'm speaking now from ubuzali* (being the parent).

Caring and sharing resources are both uBuntu principles P7 indicated displayed these principles in the following:

You know it is very sad sometimes I don't know what to do, I don't know what to do I have taken, I do that a lot during winter I transport my clients (pause) no taxis during that time it's raining, cold I am getting to my car I drive away, sometimes it's very sad and I leave my clients behind and I leave them unattended and how are you going feel? It is not nice, so uBuntu is to take this person home; it is going compromise you because you going arrive late at home but this person will be much safer.

This quote is a demonstration of a dilemma and confusion faced by practitioners who sometimes due to the strict guidelines of psychology would feel that they are directed to act in what appears to be an inhumane way. uBuntu would prescribe that the practitioner shows more humanity. Clients want to see that practitioners care.

5.7.2.6 uBuntu misrepresentation

As noted in the previous sections, uBuntu is largely constructed by participants as positive behaviour that is displayed through sharing, respect among others. As positive as it seems, ways in which people interpret uBuntu can lead to problems. P2 indicated:

... another issue is that I had is when people have a sense of entitlement, I kinda want to break that tradition... uBuntu also has boundaries, what are we teaching our children? So it sounds as if they are entitles to do anything and everything, so there's got to be some limits and where sometimes you say 'no' you mean it.

Another example of misrepresentation of uBuntu is that sometimes other people become abusive to others who have maybe share their resources with them in the past as an act of uBuntu. The recipient of uBuntu practice may demand to always receive and do nothing to be in a position of being a giver as well. P5 indicated that while she was acting on uBuntu and gave a client a CD to assist in the challenge the client had, the client never returned her CD. This illustrates how a gesture of kindness might not be reciprocated.

P1 explained another imperfection of uBuntu:

uBuntu, it's like going an extra mile to show uBuntu... it is going an extra mile. bendiyithetha ba kokwakucreater idependancy (maybe it is going to what I mentioned earlier, that thing of creating dependency).

This means that practices of uBuntu can diminish the autonomy of people, when the idea is to receive from others until you can be independent, so you can assist others who are not yet independent.

Another example is the challenges of seeing clients outside the traditional psychotherapy space as an act of uBuntu, compromising certain ethics such as privacy and confidentiality. In other words, although seeing clients in other spaces may seem acceptable in uBuntu practises, some uBuntu practitioners are not comfortable with that. P3 shares her discomfort:

> *... there is some kind of privacy, ya it won't be like in the practice, but that one at home there was no privacy I didn't feel comfortable at all. I mean anyone can just come and knock I think after some time the child came from wherever, ya it was not conducive.*

To conclude, in my analysis I have five superordinate themes discussed above; which are intertwined and connected to each other in some way. They indicate that socialisation of people influences the way people behave. This way of behaviour is observed in the way psychologists practise psychotherapy whether they adhere or not to the set guidelines of psychotherapy. Therapy frames on the other hand enhance the way psychotherapy is practised. They are not too rigid and therefore are accommodative of practitioners that are not of European origin such as amaXhosa whose core value is uBuntu. It seems as though uBuntu practises in psychotherapy increases the success rate of psychotherapy although it is not without faults. In the nutshell, these therapy frames, ethics as well as uBuntu are all constructed by humans, therefore they can be challenged, improved or reconstructed in order to be relevant to where they are practised.

CHAPTER 6

DISCUSSION

6.1 Introduction

In this chapter I discuss how I have addressed the gaps that exist in the literature review and incorporate my findings. I interpret and describe the significance of my findings, while responding to my research questions in an attempt to discuss the experiences of psychotherapists regarding uBuntu in their psychotherapy practice. This chapter is divided into four sections according to my research questions as they appear in chapter 3.

6.1.1 The foundational principles and ethics of psychotherapy

In this section I respond to research question 1 stated in chapter 3 by focusing on the original principles and ethics at the basis of psychotherapy that seem to raise recurring problems and cause dissonance for psychotherapists of African origin.

The original principles and ethics of psychotherapy for South Africans are the ones indicated by Steere and Wassenaar (1985) (see section 2.5.1): autonomy, non-maleficence and beneficence, justice, fidelity and responsibility. These original principles are concerned with the freedom of choice of the individual, the safety of the individual and acting in the best interest of the individual. These principles were derived from a different culture and context from that of the amaXhosa or people of African origin, and are embedded in Western approaches. These fundamental ethical principles seem to raise recurring problems for psychotherapists of African origin in that they focus on the individual instead of the family, community or society. The participants in the study noted that the principles were confining, seemed impersonal and did not resonate with their humanity. Literature and my data note that interdependence is one of the major virtues in African culture. In other words, an individual is not perceived as an isolated unit but as part of a community. In this regard Oppenheim (2012) noted that only through harmonious integration into one's community of others can oneself become more genuinely human.

Participants alluded to the interconnectedness they experience with their clients while in practice. They reflected on the way they drew on their experiences as parents, adults or relatives and how this influenced their responses. African interconnectedness, as illustrated in the literature review chapter, involves the belief that a child is raised by a community. Perceiving clients as strangers for African psychotherapists is uncomfortable and does not help in psychotherapy for both parties.

The autonomy of an African person is different from that of a person of European origin. For example, a person that has come of age in the European culture leaves home to rent a flat and start her own life; in a sense she is experiencing her autonomy. However, African autonomy involves others; because one has been helped by family members to gain life achievements, one then needs to uplift others in the family. Family will always be connected to an individual and vice versa. This is highlighted by the interview conducted by journalist Tim Modise with tata Nelson Mandela in 2006 (cited in Oppenheim, 2012:369):

> A traveller through a country would stop at a village and he didn't have to ask for food or for water. Once he stops, the people give him food, entertain him. That is one aspect of uBuntu, but it will have various aspects. uBuntu does not mean that people should not enrich themselves. The question therefore is: Are you going to do so in order to enable the community around you to be able to improve?

This highlights the inherent interdependence of people, foregrounded in ways of being, belonging and behaving. Psychotherapy is, in general, viewed through Western lenses and not the lenses of uBuntu.

With respect to non-maleficence, ideas of respect and disrespect come to mind. What seems to be harmful to Western people may not be harmful to amaXhosa and vice versa. For example, the amaXhosa child does not address adults by their first names; one is called by one's clan name such as *uSbewu* or *uMamgqwashu* (clan name) or by one's profession such as *umfundisi* (reverend) *utitshala* (teacher) or the town one lives in such as '*utata'se Kapa*' (a father who lives in Cape Town). When it comes to a relationship between the client and a therapist, they could both use any of these ways of addressing someone. Sometimes calling a client '*mntana'm*' (my child) seems warm and brings an element of interrelatedness and may be helpful in psychotherapy signifying *intlonipho/ukuhlonipha* (respect). It can be uncomfortable for both the therapist and the client if this element of uBuntu is absent in psychotherapy sessions.

In my findings, participants alluded to an experience of dissonance when their clients brought gifts as tokens of appreciation that they were expected (by the profession) to reject as it was unethical to accept gifts from clients. Rejecting a gift is perceived as rejecting the gift bearer. They also reported giving bus fares to clients or being given chocolate or a book. Rejecting gifts is potentially harmful to both client and psychotherapist. Though participants broke this ethical rule, they did so with so much dissonance. However, this positive gesture can be abused by both parties and needs further discussion in the profession. I suggest these discussions should include the issue of psychotherapists giving gifts to clients. Participants mentioned both giving and lending items (such as CDs and books) to clients which were very useful to them.

My research also explored participants going 'the extra mile' to assist their clients. It is a norm among amaXhosa that the one who has resources goes the extra mile to assist the one who has less and this is one example of uBuntu. It therefore can be harmful to both client and therapist if there is unwillingness to go the extra mile. Participants indicated that they are expected to spend a therapeutic hour or more with their clients even when clients were late for their sessions. The feeling of incongruity experienced by participants when doing what comes naturally to them was disturbing to them.

Regarding beneficence, what may be perceived as in the best interest of the client in the European sense may not be in the best interest of the African client. Refusing to give advice to an African client may be perceived as not in the best interest of the client. In isiXhosa for example, *inyathi'ibuzwa kwabaphambili* means one can ask for directions from the knowledgeable. My research showed that clients often asked participants to advise them on certain decisions. In Eurocentric psychotherapy therapists are discouraged from giving advice to clients but in the African way of living, adults are expected to give advice to youngsters.

Oppenheim (2012) noted that Mandela highlighted the multi-faceted nature of uBuntu as an innate duty to support one's fellow humans. In this regard giving to the client what the client needs is perceived as supportive. Participants expressed their fears when practising a perceived duty to support fellow humans, which brought tensions for both clients and participants.

As indicated in chapter 2, justice refers to equal and fair distribution of mental health benefits to those in need. In the case of South Africa this is far from being achieved due to the legacy of Apartheid. South Africa can be regarded as two worlds in one (both first and third worlds) with those that are privileged (i.e. the less than 20% of people who are on medical aids) who get the best medical, psychological and psychiatric attention in well managed medical facilities while those that are under-resourced (mostly Blacks due to previous oppression) do not have medical aids nor financial resources to pay for psychological and psychiatric services in facilities that are accessible. Their only access is to public psychiatric facilities where there are long queues and waiting lists. Such African clients are also dependent on other people for transport to those facilities. Psychotherapists of African origin understand these circumstances and the interdependence that their clients value.

Not to lend a helping hand in any way possible causes confusion to psychotherapists of African origin. Lending a helping hand could be in a form of sharing bus fare, food, or advice. I perceive these uBuntu gestures as partially striving to correct what seems unjust; which in my view is another way of interpreting the meaning of justice. The poor socio-economic backgrounds of many African clients caused participants to share personal resources with them, which may be perceived in the Eurocentric view as creating dependency. These clashing perceptions of uBuntu and Western views causes tensions for participants. Clients should all be treated equally and be given equal treatment for the same challenges regardless of their race, colour or creed. I wonder how far this equal treatment of everyone takes place in the very unequal South Africa that continues to be influenced by Apartheid elements in almost all areas, including mental health services.

Fidelity and responsibility refer to psychotherapists' loyalties and accountability. An African client is regarded as an individual client as well as part of a family and community. Even though psychotherapists work with an individual, that individual is a representative of the family and community, the living and the dead. If a psychotherapist ignores those other important elements of this individual, psychotherapy may fail. Welfel and Leach (2018) noted that negative judgments and fear of violating boundaries may lead to psychotherapists isolating themselves rather than seeking the support needed to act responsibly. Participants reported that behaving in a way that would be hurtful to clients while ostensibly behaving in a responsible manner confused them in terms of their loyalties. Dissonance appears to be caused in participants who are trying to be loyal to both their clients and to the HPCSA by feelings of having to choose one over the other. Van Stam (cited in Mawere & Mabuya, 2016) noted that uBuntu signifies human solidarity and is explicitly against inequality or isolating individualism.

To conclude this section, these fundamental ethical principles seem relevant to psychotherapists of African origin but need to be augmented to suit the way of living of amaXhosa, for them to be useful in psychotherapy. Participants noted the difficulties that arose due to the dissonance experienced by participants who were amaXhosa psychotherapists that had been socialised differently from the originators of psychology. Participants reflected on the frustration experienced when practising in a way that is different from the way they had been socialised.

In the following section I continue to respond to the first research question, but focus on the practical ethical principles and regulations of professional conduct as suggested by Steere and Wassenaar (1985). In other words I respond to how these practical ethical principles cause dissonance among psychotherapists of African origin. One of the reasons for such dissonances is due to the fact that psychology of Africans involves human behaviour and minds in their 'natural context' (Lawson, Graham and Baker cited in Mkabela, 2015). The natural context refers here to the way of living of Africans and how they are socialised.

6.1.2 Practical ethical principles and regulations for professional conduct

In this section I focus on the practical principles and regulations for professional conduct. These principles include professional responsibility, social responsibility, informed consent, confidentiality, competence and welfare of the client (Steere & Wassenaar, 1985). These imply that a psychotherapist, as a professional, is expected to behave in a certain way. This behaviour would be influenced by the way one is socialised and a person of European origin is socialised differently from an African.

6.1.2.1 Professional responsibility

Professional responsibility means that one is accountable to professional bodies for one's actions. Such actions may include autonomy where practitioner respects the right of individuals to make their own decisions. In some cases a client comes to consult because she needs someone to make a decision for her. This may cause dissonance in African psychotherapists whose professional training discourages them from taking away the autonomy of the client, while in the African culture it is common practice to make decisions or give advice to influence a decision for those in need, particularly children or those who are vulnerable. Applying European related autonomy to an African client may be experienced as a disservice to an African client and may be confusing to psychotherapists of African origin.

The professional bodies that psychotherapists are accountable to implement Eurocentric psychotherapy rules and regulations, in which uBuntu or African ways of life are not prioritised. This leads to misunderstanding of certain professional behaviours of African psychotherapists. It is the professional responsibility of every psychotherapist to be immersed in the different cultures in the area in which he/she practises. Participants exhibited frustration caused by misunderstandings which are a result of cultural clashes. This frustration leads to psychotherapists of African origin wanting to practise psychotherapy differently from the way they feel forced to, rigidly following Eurocentric principles. Psychotherapy is meant to help or heal those in need but it is frustrating to psychotherapists of African origin and to their clients to practise in a way that does not bring healing because of compliance with rules of the professional body. Professional bodies should contribute to positive mental health rather than enforcing rules.

6.1.2.2 Social responsibility

In terms of social responsibility, both the individual and society are important. The psychotherapist is expected to behave professionally and this behaviour perceived in Western way of living involves doing things 'by the book' while the African way may involve more interconnection with the person or collective. In my view, doing things 'by the book' creates an emotional distance between individuals while interconnectedness implies working together and perceiving a person more as a person than as a subject. These differences in cultural practices may pose dissonance among psychotherapists of African origin who value interconnectedness but who feel their professional training follows Eurocentric expectations. This frustration has been exacerbated by the legacy of Apartheid in South Africa as articulated by Biko (1972) in the following quotation:

Figure 6.1: Biko on the legacy of apartheid

This quotation emphasises the need for us to be seeing the human-ness in each other without ascribing superiority or inferiority. In South Africa we need to do things in a South African way, not in the Eurocentric manner, psychotherapy included.

According to Mangena (2016) uBuntu is not a rule-based philosophy focused on explaining individual behaviour and the attendant discourse of individual rights or theory crafted by one person; rather it focuses a communal way of life as lived by the Bantu-speaking people of South Africa. For instance, in almost every Southern African village, children are socialised to value the interests and needs of the group, more than they would value their own individual interests. In my opinion, it is a responsibility of a competent psychotherapist to appreciate the values of societies in which they practise and engage in these activities of their society. I appreciate and commend community psychology for engaging in building partnerships that strive for collaboration, working together and valuing the voices of all.

6.1.2.3 Informed consent

Informed consent implies that the individual gives permission for treatment to take place. It is the adult client that must give consent, but in a case where the client is a minor, a guardian or parent can give consent on behalf of the child. In isiXhosa culture a child does not have much of a say in issues, even in those issues that pertain to the child. It is adults that make decisions for their children. Moreover, an African child is raised by the community not only by biological parents. This implies that a psychotherapist, being an adult, automatically has cultural authority to discipline or decide for the child and would not be expected to seek permission from the parents.

The rules of consent are contradictory because in South Africa 13 year old girls can terminate pregnancies without the consent of a parent or guardian, but for any psychotherapy intervention, guardians or parents need to give consent (or the psychotherapist can be charged for seeing the client without informed consent). This is one of the areas that causes dissonance among psychotherapists of African origin and I think needs further discussion by the profession.

6.1.2.4 Confidentiality

Confidentiality in an African context may also be different from a European context. In an African context sharing information within the family and at times with the extended family members may be perceived as keeping something confidential, whereas in the Western perspective, no information may be disclosed except in cases where keeping the information may cause harm to the client or others. In this case, most participants indicated that although they would like to change other Western principles, they would like to preserve confidentiality because they see its value. Although participants are of African origin, to disclose a client's information to a third party when no one is in danger of anything, caused dissonance in participants. This suggests participants would like to preserve confidentiality in the way it is currently prescribed. This illustrates that participants see the value in certain principles.

6.1.2.5 Competence

In my view, maintaining high standards of competence in the interest of the public and the profession involves knowing the different cultures a practitioner works within for the welfare of clients. For example, the welfare of the client may involve the therapist going beyond the scope of practice of the psychotherapist to assist which might be discouraged because this could be viewed as creating dependency. This 'going out of the practitioner's way' may include attending prayers during the week in the home of the client when there is death in the client's family or even attending a funeral service of the loved one of the client. This attending of prayers in the home of the client is interpreted as 'you care' or 'you feel the pain I feel' (*ungumntu* you are human). From an African perspective, a relationship between two people who have met does not end in that one meeting space, it transcends to other spaces as well. In other words, because the therapist and the client have met and spoken, they now know each other (*bayazana*). It can feel like rejection when one of the two 'pretends' not to know another in another environment, in the name of protecting the professional relationship. In such spaces of 'pretending' both the African client and psychotherapist become uncomfortable this could harm the therapeutic relationship that has been established.In this regard, clients are not trained in psychology, so in public spaces they are likely to behave 'naturally' openly displaying that they have met the psychotherapist. This can cause dissonance for psychotherapists because while they understand their clients' reasons, they are also cognisant that they are professionally discouraged from interacting with clients outside of psychotherapy space in order to protect the therapeutic relationship.

In relation to maintaining continued competence, I appreciate that psychotherapists need to keep abreast of current theories. This means attending CPD courses which can be expensive. Participants alluded to CPD courses not addressing certain issues that impact on the mental health of clients, such as economic issues. Professional ethics are important, as are courses to develop and maintain these, but they do not address every challenge that one experiences in practice, hence I think one's competence in the field cannot be limited to how one complies with the rules of ethics. Welfel and Leach (2018) noted that attending courses does not necessarily ensure ethical behaviour and is sometimes an act of mere compliance.

6.1.2.6 Welfare of the client

Welfare of the client is linked to principles of non-maleficence and beneficence. In my view amaXhosa participants of this study experienced dissonance because their clients found it difficult to understand and accept certain ways of conduct, suggested by their therapists.

My question regarding the welfare of the client is: Whose welfare are amaXhosa psychotherapists' concerned about? Are they concerned about their own professional welfare or their clients? If they claim to be concerned about their client's welfare then they will find tensions in certain Western principles for people socialised in the African way of living. It seems as if African people must change their cultural beliefs for them to benefit from psychotherapy. Surely this view is not person-centred. It also seems to be contradicting the very values psychotherapy professes to uphold. It is not in the best interests of the client to 'enforce' 'strange' ideas or behaviours. It is harmful to an individual seeking help to find that one is socialised in a way that is not acceptable in psychology, as may be experienced in current practices. These differences of culture and profession are perplexing and frustrating to psychotherapists of African origin. The frustrations experienced by psychotherapists are directed towards the HPCSA, perceived as the enforcer of these regulations. Although the psychotherapist's main concern is to ensure that the client's needs are properly met, she worries that her uBuntu-related methods are not conventional.

Psychotherapists of African origin are aware of ethical principles and regulations and strive to comply with HPCSA for fear of being charged or deregistered. Often this is under duress as some of these ethical principles and regulations do not work adequately in practice for

Africans. This needs to be further discussed by the profession and should be properly regulated, to be context relevant. To relate naturally, both the therapist and the client need to interact based on their socialisation processes. The interconnectedness of body, soul, spirit, behaviours in natural lived contexts challenges atomistic processes, when the whole person is foregrounded as in an African context.

6.1.3 uBuntu principles applicable to psychotherapy practice

In this section I respond to research question 2, as indicated in section 3.12 namely: What uBuntu principles are applicable to psychotherapy practice experienced by psychotherapists? This research question is in line with the style of living of the amaXhosa. Due to the fact that the Western principles of psychotherapy addressed by research question 1 do not fully accommodate Africans, research question 2 is designed to suggest principles of psychotherapy that could work for amaXhosa psychotherapists in their practice. Mkabela (2015) argued that uBuntu locates psychology from an African viewpoint and creates Africa's own intellectual perspective by insiders. As an insider I view individuals holistically, the body soul and spirit in psychotherapy and this study is designed to create our own intellectual property regarding psychotherapy.

These need to be further discussed by the profession and need to be properly regulated, to be context relevant. Expanded ethical principles as described in section 2.5.3 are privacy, integrity, tolerance, respect for persons, compassion, truthfulness, community. These expanded ethical principles are mostly similar to principles of uBuntu and may not cause dissonance or may even be understood better by African psychologists.

Some of the uBuntu principles are implicit in HPCSA ethical regulations. These principles include tolerance, compassion and community, all of which are closely related to interdependence. Integrity, fidelity and responsibility are some of the ethical principles that are stipulated in the HPCSA regulations and in principles of uBuntu. Respect is one of the HPCSA ethical regulations resonating with the Rogerian Person/Client Centred Approach (Corey, 2005) – respect is one of its cornerstones and is also one of the uBuntu values as described in section 3.3.2.

My findings indicate a number of uBuntu principles that seem to be applicable to psychotherapy: interdependence, respect, going the extra-mile, spirituality, sharing, caring, humility, selflessness, receiving and giving gifts, bartering, appropriate touching and dignity. In the following sub-sections I explain how I think these principles could be used when treating amaXhosa in psychotherapy.

6.1.3.1 Interdependence

Interdependence is one of the core values of uBuntu that seem to be important across different age groups of clients. Enquiring about clan and ancestry is not inappropriate in amaXhosa culture as establishment of blood links tends to enable greater levels of trust between the client and the psychotherapist. This involves sharing of clan names and personal information about the psychotherapist with the client, viewed as inappropriate according to Western ethical regulations. For example, an older client may ask what is your clan name, *iphi inkaba yakho?* (where were you born/where is your home?) in trying to establish these blood links. Mawere and Mabuya (2016) express this as *Ubu* and *ntu* constituting a wholeness and oneness. In my view, this means an individual is not complete without uniting with others. Another example of interdependence is illustrated in psychotherapy sessions by a younger client who may ask questions such as: Are you from this town? Is so and so your daughter or related to you? This could be a way of establishing rapport. Refusing to engage with questions like these that seem personal may alienate clients and prevent the therapeutic relationship from flowing smoothly. Participants highlighted the success of their therapeutic relations with clients when there was a deep understanding and trust of each other and the feeling that they could depend on each other.

Western clients tend to choose to consult with psychotherapists they do not know. When they do consult, they talk about their problems and do not seem to seek for any interconnections with the psychotherapist. Mawere and Mabuya (2016) noted that uBuntu is a concrete manifestation of the interconnectedness of human beings and a core value of an African culture and lifestyle which focuses on holism.

Psychotherapists could be flexible and ask the same questions asked by the client to indicate their interest in the client as a person. Interdependence can include sharing of personal information of a psychotherapist with a client.

6.1.3.2 Respect

According to Mkabela (2015), respect is an act of demonstrating that someone or something is valuable, important, and good and should be treated appropriately. In the context of uBuntu respect is stressed as important from childhood and is characterised by humility, empathy, maturity, hospitality, politeness and understanding. amaXhosa psychotherapists would want to preserve respect *(intlonipho)* as one of the values in their psychotherapy practice. The Eurocentric Client Centred Approach has respect as one of its principles, however amaXhosa respect is practised differently. An examples is that in isiXhosa it shows respect not to look someone in the eye when talking particularly if that person is older than oneself. I believe that in the Western perspective not to look someone in the eye when talking is regarded as something negative. In isiXhosa respect involves not calling someone older or with more authority or a higher status by name; one uses a prefixes such as *mam'u-* (mother-), *tat'u-* (father-), bhut'- (brother-), sis'- (sister -) with the person's name. The use of idioms when talking about someone is also perceived as a sign of respect in isiXhosa traditions. For example when referring to a young man that displays negative behaviour similar to his father's, a therapist may say *igqabi aliwi kude emthini* interpreted as 'you take after your father'. In another case where a father is well-respected but the son is always in trouble one might say *umthathi uyawuzala umlotha* ('a strong tree becomes useless ashes'). In other words respect is one of the attributes that amaXhosa psychotherapists would want to preserve but in a manner that accommodates isiXhosa traditions.

6.1.3.3 Spirituality

According to Mbiti (1991) African people are very religious, which could imply that everything African has religion as its base. Corey (2005) indicated that spirituality has become part of psychology that cannot be ignored because it is that which connects us to other people, nature and sources of life. Spirituality or religion is also greater than ourselves and assists us in transcending and embracing different life situations. Mkabela (2015) indicated that psychologists that blindly adopt imported foreign theories may fall into ethnocentrism using concepts that are foreign to people of African origin. An example would be a client with *amafufunyana* may not be understood by people that are not of African origin and may therefore be misdiagnosed which leads to mis-treatment and therefore no healing will take place. Another example of ethnocentrism is a person with *ubizo* (calling) may be perceived as someone who is hallucinating in Eurocentric psychology but a psychotherapist of African origin may understand the symptoms and be able to assist the client better. Empathy and cultural understanding is required from the psychotherapist.

Sometimes clients with symptoms of *ubizo*, *ukutwasa, amafufunyana* may be seeing diviners or traditional healers but have emotional issues pertaining to their symptoms that they need to help with. This may require a psychotherapist that understands how these work in order to properly assist the client. A psychotherapist that has been socialised in environments or rather in social situations that accommodate such behaviours or beliefs may understand these clients better.

Clients sometimes prefer to consult folk healers when experiencing symptoms that seem not to be understood by psychologists. Helman (1990) indicated the importance of understanding the world around a client who is at the centre. There is the natural world or the circumstances of a client. This is followed by the social world that has important associations. These worlds, namely client, natural and social are governed by the supernatural world. It is crucial to foreground this knowledge for better and quicker results.

uBuntu principles are part of the socialisation of amaXhosa psychotherapists; however their training as psychotherapists does not seem to fully accommodate certain socialisation factors of amaXhosa and this can lead to dilemmas and confusion in some situations. amaXhosa psychotherapists can feel torn between their culturally influenced perceptions and their professional training. Clients also seem to benefit more when treated in a way that accommodates their way of living.

Spirituality is a crucial element of African people but is not the same for all Africans or even all amaXhosa. *Izindlu azifani zifana ngeentlanti zodwa* (homes and rituals are not similar, they are only similar in kraals) means that even though psychotherapist and client may both be amaXhosa, they may have different beliefs; a psychotherapist needs to show interest in the beliefs of the client that are different from his/hers.

6.1.3.4 Sharing

Sharing is another principle of uBuntu that could work in psychotherapy. Participants in this study indicated that they have shared personal finances for the benefit of needy clients, personal items such as clothing, compact discs, books among other things, as well as information that clients were perhaps supposed to find out on their own. Africans generally share. It is an insult in isiXhosa traditions to be selfish; when one shares personal resources such as time, listening, a skill to upgrade others, that person is regarded as *uno*Buntu (possessesing humanity). Participants in this study described various forms of sharing in their practice where they shared personal items such as CDs, books, time and some offered to do things for their clients such as collecting forms from a school. Participants also received items shared by their clients such as cake, fish, bags or chocolates. While sharing is an acceptable value of uBuntu, it could be abused and lead to corruption, therefore it should be properly managed.

6.1.3.5 Touch

A psychotherapist touching a client is taboo in Western psychotherapy. Touch is one of the ways in uBuntu that indicates that one accepts, acknowledges and is interconnected with another person. This touch is displayed in shaking hands or hugging. Some clients shake hands at the beginning of sessions; some hug a psychotherapist at the end of a session. Rejecting those uBuntu related gestures may be perceived as cold by the client. I think the issue of touch should be carefully discussed because it could be abused by both the psychotherapist and the client and become harmful. Appropriate touching is hugging and shaking of hands in a proper manner.

6.1.3.6 Gifts and bartering

In isiXhosa traditions when one needs attention from someone in a higher position, one 'brings a goat'; in other words, one comes bearing a gift. In isiXhosa this is called *ukuchamel'inkundla* (to bring a gift in order to get attention). Goats are expensive, so instead of a goat one might bring *ibhotil'eblanti* (a bottle of brandy). This bringing of a gift also applies when one wants to express one's gratitude for something. Rejecting a gift in isiXhosa is perceived as rejecting the gift bearer.

In this regard, participants indicated that although at the beginning of the therapeutic relationship they might have indicated to their clients that they are not allowed to accept gifts, clients still often left gifts after finishing a session. Participants received handbags, compact discs, chocolates, fried fish or cake, among other things. Some of these gifts were not given to participants directly, but were left with the receptionist. Although participants accepted the gifts from their clients, they did not consume these gifts as they felt guilty and as if, by doing so, they would not be complying with HPCSA regulations. Some gave the gifts to their relatives, receptionists or colleagues. This giving away or consuming the gift with others as well as the time spent justifying reasons for accepting gifts, indicated the dissonance/discomfort the gifts caused them as psychotherapists trained in the Western tradition. This aspect of therapy could be properly regulated for positive results and should not risk leading to corruption.

Receiving gifts in the South African context is not the challenge of health professionals only; it seems a challenge in government institutions as well. This means it is an important issue that should not be ignored. The HPCSA could be influenced by the SA Public Service Commission (PSC) to regulate the acceptance of gifts from clients and the giving of gifts to clients. The following excerpt indicates that the policies in South Africa have been influenced by the Western way of living since democratic government policies have been revised to reflect all people of South Africa.

> The Code of Conduct for the Public Service places a prohibition on the receiving of gifts in the Public Service. However, irrespective of the prohibition by the Code of Conduct it is a fact of life that public servants are constantly being showered with gifts, sometimes even without the public servant having the opportunity of refusal, e.g. gifts delivered by courier. There is also a persistent argument that gifts from an Afro-centric perspective has grey areas as in most cultures it is deemed unacceptable not to accept a gift. Therefore, the receipt of gifts could be regarded as a highly emotive issue… destroying the fibre of integrity and good corporate governance within the Public Service. Moreover, it compromises the idea of having an ethically sound… it is recommended that should a public servant receive a gift based on a cultural tradition it should be treated and managed in a culturally sensitive manner without compromising the standards of accountability and transparency. Importantly, the public servant should disclose such a gift in line with the gift policy applicable to the relevant department. Should a public servant decide not to receive the gift he/she may request the person or community offering the gift to show appreciation by submitting a letter of commendation to the said public servant's superior or EA. (PSC, 2008, ii & 34)

Most people from disadvantaged backgrounds cannot afford to pay cash for costly psychotherapy sessions, but they may have something else to offer for the sessions. The inability to pay for sessions means psychotherapy becomes inaccessible to Black clients who do not have medical aids. Although none of the participants in this research referred to bartering as a means to pay for sessions, ways to make psychological services more accessible need to be explored. To conclude this section, to reject a gift from a client could do more harm to a person that has come for healing. The issue of gifts needs to be debated further by the profession.

6.1.3.7 Caring, humility, selflessness, compassion

These are some of uBuntu principles that need to be incorporated into psychotherapy that sometimes leave psychotherapists unsettled and confused. In isiXhosa *ukukhathala* (caring) for the well-being of others is a crucial part of healing. For example, in cases where someone falls ill and is hospitalised, the behaviour of the nurse in the hospital sometimes becomes as important as the medication. One might say *bendiphetheke kakuhle oonurse bebekhathala bendihoyile, ndatsho ndaphila msinya* ('I was taken good care of; nurses took good care of me that is why I recovered quicker'). In other words, when practitioners show signs of caring for the client this increases chances of quicker recovery.

Ukuthobeka (humility) means having a modest view of ones' importance, which is crucial in uBuntu and makes one feel accepted, respected and loved by people. This attribute is perceived as one's ability to be reachable by a greater community to assist those in need. This is also perceived as the ability to be able to come 'down' to the level of those who are 'down'. 'Down' is perceived as having 'nothing', nothing means 'having few things' which keeps one humble. Wealthy people are perceived as conceited. A humble psychotherapist is approachable, reachable and this facilitates the healing of a client.
Selflessness is the opposite of selfish. In isiXhosa it is an insult to be perceived as a selfish person. One gains more respect in the community if one is perceived as a selfless person who helps others who have less, to the extent of using personal resources such as time, car, home, or stationery.

When one displays such attributes in isiXhosa one is perceived as having *ububele* (warmth), one of the attributes of uBuntu. Compassion, according to HPCSA (2008), means healthcare practitioners should be sensitive to, and empathise with the individual and social needs of their clients and seek to create mechanisms for providing comfort and support where appropriate and possible.

These are uBuntu values and therapy frames that do not harm psychotherapists nor clients that could be beneficial if used in the best interest of the therapy relationship. I conclude this section by quoting Mawere and Mabuya (2016:99) who indicate that uBuntu has the potential to "rescue African people from their loss of identity: to let them regain their cultural and social values and to let them experience themselves as human beings with dignity".

6.1.4 The experiences of psychotherapists regarding incorporating uBuntu into their practice

The third research question was designed to elucidate the experiences of amaXhosa psychotherapists when they used some principles of the amaXhosa style of living: What are the experiences of psychotherapists regarding incorporating uBuntu into their practice? Incorporating uBuntu in practice is currently not experienced as positive but rather psychotherapists are fearful of professional judgements when reported to HPCSA either by colleagues or clients. Experiences of participants regarding incorporating uBuntu into their practice are discussed under topics such as 'African time', giving advice, flexibility in the setting, normalising, psychoeducation, language and culture, poor socio-economic backgrounds, privacy and informed consent as well as rapport.

6.1.4.1 African time

This refers to a more relaxed attitude towards time than what is common in Western traditions, and which manifests itself in the lateness of clients for their psychotherapy appointments. In the isiXhosa way of living there is not much emphasis on time. Participants noted that their clients 'practised African time' in that they would be late for their sessions and then still expect to have a full hour session. Participants experienced discomfort in clients coming late for sessions; others justified their clients coming late by indicating that they might have had transport challenges because of public transport. This lateness is an accepted phenomenon in most African contexts, even though it is viewed as unprofessional in the West. Most participants indicated that the way they approach African time depends on whether another client is waiting for the next session. If there is a client waiting, participants find the courage to tell the current client that she needs to leave. However, if no other client is waiting they would continue with the session beyond the hour. Clients do not expect to be charged for the extra minutes. This can manifest as the 'African time syndrome' as discussed in section 5.3.1. I think the 'African time' phenomenon is a reality and needs to be looked into and accommodated or it may cause elements of maleficence.

6.1.4.2 Giving advice

amaXhosa psychotherapists say their amaXhosa clients generally want advice. It is the way of life to ask for advice from the elders, which applies to anyone who seems knowledgeable in a certain field. There is described in an isiXhosa idiom: *inyathi ibuzwa kwabaphambili* (you get the direction from people that know better than you). The Eurocentric way of practising prohibits psychotherapists from giving advice to their clients lest clients hold them accountable should the advice not work well. Dissonance may be caused by the difference between the expected professional conduct and the culture of both the client and psychotherapist. Clients might feel dissatisfied if they are not given advice while according to the profession, clients shows growth by being able to make sound decisions on their own. Participants feared giving advice to clients for the fear that this might backfire, however in some cases such as rape, domestic violence, they did give advice for they felt it would be harmful to their clients not to. While the research participants did give advice to clients they felt uncomfortable due to the influence of Eurocentric psychology. I think advice could be negotiated with the client if the client is comfortable with the advice given, in the same way in which homework is negotiated with clients.

6.1.4.3 Flexibility

In terms of flexibility, amaXhosa psychotherapists indicated that they felt it did not assist them to be rigid when it comes to the behaviour of clients particularly outside of the therapy space. Even though ground rules are discussed at the beginning of the therapy relationship, clients break these rules and this puts psychotherapists in an uncomfortable position. On one hand, they understand what is expected of them in terms of their practice; on the other hand, they understand how amaXhosa function. Participants indicated that they understood when clients discussed issues for sessions outside the therapeutic space and they wanted to help and are not trained nor socialised in Western principles. They did not know how to handle such situations; ignoring a client because it is out of therapeutic space may be perceived as a rejection and an element of *ukuphakama* (being conceited) which creates a gap between client and psychotherapist. Yet discussing sensitive issues publicly jeopardises confidentiality and privacy.

6.1.4.4 The setting: Taking the service to the people

Literature tells us that uBuntu traditional spaces include *iziko* (the centre of a rondavel where the fire is made in African homes) and *ngasebuhlanti* (next to the kraal). None of the research participants felt this kind of setting would be suitable for conducting sessions. This may be due to the fact that I conducted all interviews in urban and semi-urban areas of the Eastern Cape, where there are no kraals and *amaziko*. None of the participants suggested an alternate space for practising psychotherapy.

Participants indicated that they saw their clients mostly in their rooms which were designed in a traditional fashion, with a couch, closed door, enough ventilation and so on. However, they were flexible, seeing clients wherever it was convenient for both of them. It seemed the psychotherapists perhaps had more of an issue about where sessions should take place as clients do not seem worried about where they could talk or be heard. Psychotherapists seemed to be cognisant of confidentiality and privacy issues when they see clients outside of traditional therapy space, though some indicated that they saw clients in coffee shops, hospitals, homes, among other spaces.

6.1.4.5 Normalising

It seems it is important for African clients to be 'normal' because it is an insult if one is said to be not normal. One with psychiatric challenges is called *igeza* or *uyaphambana,* meaning crazy or abnormal. This is one of the reasons psychological services are stigmatised. For example, in Makhanda and in Queenstown where there are very efficient psychiatric hospitals, people call them *emagezeni* (a place for mad, crazy people). Thus, people are cautious of being associated with any illness that has the potential to lead them to institutions such as Komani Mental Health or Fort England Hospital. It is therefore important to normalise the experience of psychotherapy. Participants indicated that they could use personal experiences to normalise difficult situations facing their clients. Participants felt prohibited from doing this because of their training and if they did, they feared the law. One participant normalised by externalising, for example she would indicate to a couple: 'it is your marriage that needs to be fixed but you and your wife are fine'. In other words normalising reflects caring, empathy and non-judgment which are all attributes of uBuntu. This means normalising is a therapy frame that can be useful in psychotherapy with amaXhosa clients.

6.1.4.6 Psychoeducation

According to Gelso, Williams and Fretz (2014), psychoeducation is a preventative intervention to envision the development of problems. Psychotherapists in this research all aimed to educate their clients about psychotherapy processes and mental health. This was conducted with individual clients and with groups at any stage of the therapeutic process but mostly at the beginning. I think this is because psychology is a Western profession and it is a relatively new phenomenon for African people. Participants found psychoeducation helpful in their interaction with their clients. It was interesting to note that participants did not fear HPCSA when they psycho-educated their clients, possibly as they did not feel they were challenging the law when they psycho-educated individuals or groups.

6.1.4.7 Language and culture

Language is an important part of psychotherapy because people use verbal and non-verbal cues to communicate in psychotherapy. Most participants indicated that they used their vernacular [isiXhosa in this case] to communicate with their clients. However, with the younger generation and educated groups, they mixed isiXhosa and English. Language transcends the spoken word in that to understand certain cultural practices one needs to understand the client's worldview. Consulting with the psychotherapist that understands the culture of the client creates a better understanding between the client and the therapist. It may be a tool for speeding up the development of rapport.

Language can also be used to show respect which is one of the crucial elements of uBuntu and a Client Centred Approach. For example, even though amaXhosa males do not consult as much as females do, when they do they expect to be respected by not being called by their first names particularly if the therapist is younger or female. This is how amaXhosa males are socialised. It is perceived as being 'womanish' or weak to talk about problems, particularly to strangers. To discourage males from seeking help or talk about challenges there is an isiXhosa proverb: *indod'ayikhali* (men do not cry). Men feel respected if they are called Mr or addressed by their clan names. Thus psychotherapists working with amaXhosa male clients should be culturally competent.

6.1.4.8 Poor socio-economic backgrounds

amaXhosa psychotherapists experience the impoverished socio-economic backgrounds of amaXhosa in the Eastern Cape Province, partly due to the legacy of apartheid where the poor have become poorer. High percentage rates of educated youth do not find employment. Most households survive on old age government grants or one member may be employed as a domestic or general workers due to lack of formal education (during Apartheid education was not compulsory for African children).

Linked to the issue of poor socio-economic backgrounds, psychological services are costly and few can afford to pay for the services. Some clients are referred by the Employee Wellness Programmes (EWP) of their companies and then the company pays for the services. The EWP sometimes does not provide food or transport for their employees, and sometimes they travel from other towns. Some students who consult come from very poor socio-economic backgrounds where a grandmother may support the entire household with her government grant, which is not much. This causes dissonance among psychotherapists who work with these students or EWP clients. Some psychotherapists indicated that they shared clothes, food, bus fare, and money to buy food, books, informative CDs, among other things, with their clients who could not afford to buy these items. amaXhosa psychotherapists are socialised to share, care, and help where needed but in Eurocentric psychotherapy this is prohibited lest it cause dependency on clients. In certain cases, this behaviour from psychotherapists may cause dependency, but in other cases it may help bring immediate relief and give clients the necessary strength to go forward. For example, one student that was given clothes to wear at university by a psychotherapist graduated and was then able to provide for her family. Psychotherapists indicated that when they provided this kind of help to needy clients, they felt guilty because they thought their actions were unethical but also good as they had helped a fellow human who was in need. This is an example of the dissonance African psychotherapists experience in practice.

Situations of 'Black tax' (supporting the family financially) or when an adult resides at home to support his family may be perceived with Eurocentric lenses as lacking self-development, while it is understood and appreciated in an isiXhosa tradition that one must be left at home to look after *imfuyo* (livestock) and to maintain the house. This may be one of the dilemmas for amaXhosa psychotherapists as this kind behaviour may be viewed as dependence in some Western traditions and may be discouraged.

6.1.4.9 Privacy and informed consent

amaXhosa psychotherapists indicated they would choose to adhere to the principles of privacy and informed consent. The African way of functioning is largely communal, people share almost everything. In other words, if you have I also have, there seems to be no much space to be given to an individual to do private things in that your things are my things. An issue is kept private if it is discussed among the trusted members of the family but as soon as it goes beyond the family boundaries, there is no privacy.

Psychotherapy involves giving space to an individual to share what they wish in a private space where one can talk about challenges regarding this sharing of everything or expectations of the family on the individual and so forth. Even though literature refers to practising psychotherapy in other spaces such as hospitals and homes of clients, amaXhosa psychotherapists would like to preserve 'Eurocentric' privacy but be flexible to look at other spaces should the need arise. Participants indicated that although in uBuntu spaces privacy involves others, they preferred to preserve the Eurocentric meaning of privacy in their practice.

In cases of informed consent, amaXhosa psychotherapists wanted the individual coming for sessions to agree to embark on the process instead of being forced by her family.

6.1.4.10 Rapport

Rapport with a psychotherapist is essential for clients to feel comfortable before they are able to talk. amaXhosa psychotherapists indicated that rapport was important, however isiXhosa rapport differs from the Western way in that it can involve touching such as shaking hands or hugging. A therapist may also need to talk about other things for a short while such as finding the office or the traffic in order to start developing a rapport.

Rapport may also require older clients asking personal questions of psychotherapists such as *ungumni?* (what is your clan name?), *uzalwa ngumabani?* (what is your mother's clan name?) *iphi inkaba yakho?* (where were you born?) In other words, the Eurocentric value in psychotherapy of non-disclosure of personal information to clients causes a dilemma in amaXhosa psychotherapists as they sometimes feel confused as to whether to respond to such personal questions or not. Responding positively to such questions may be the beginning of a successful psychotherapy relationship which may lead to the healing of the client, whereas refusing to respond may result in a lack of trust.

Rapport for amaXhosa also included offering clients a glass of water, coffee, tea or juice as a standard procedure and that was believed to make clients feel welcomed and cared for. For example, a client indicated as a mother and a lecturer at a university, she always takes care of other people such as her husband, her children and her students – being offered a cup of coffee makes her feel that someone is taking care of her.

To conclude, this section has discussed the experiences of psychotherapists regarding incorporating uBuntu in their practice. Participants came up with certain therapy frames and principles that are common among amaXhosa that they feel should be included in the ethics of conducting psychotherapy. Such therapy frames and principles as discussed in this section are African time, giving advice, flexibility, being flexible about the setting (space), considering language and culture of the amaXhosa, in addition to being considerate of the amaXhosa's generally poor socio-economic background. Other therapy frames that participants would like preserved or changed only slightly include rapport, normalising and psychoeducation. Moreover, participants wanted to preserve privacy, informed consent and confidentiality as they are in Eurocentric psychotherapy.

6.2 Recommendations in relation to incorporating uBuntu into psychotherapy

This section responds to research question 4, namely: What can the study recommend in relation to incorporating uBuntu into psychotherapy? This research question aimed to develop principles of psychotherapy that are suitable for Africans as derived from the experiences of the participants of this study. I start by discussing these principles of therapy frames, thereafter I suggest a psychotherapy model that could work for psychotherapists of African origin.

It seems as though multicultural competencies in HPCSA and training are missing. In both HPCSA regulations and in training, cultural sensitivity or awareness need to be foregrounded knowledge and skills regarding these need to be incorporated (Leach et al, 2010). According to Johnson and Sandhu (2010), it is recommended that psychotherapists be flexible in their approach to treatment that should be adapted to meet the needs of the individual clients and that should capitalise on cultural strengths. Such treatment adaptations might include reduction of jargon, use of a different language in psychotherapy, incorporating cultural, religious and other alternative healing strategies into treatments or the use of a complete system of cultural values or frameworks to undergird techniques. Psychologists can become so immersed in standard practice that they may not perceive these important multicultural values.

It is obvious that psychology is still largely Western although it is practised with Africans; as such it needs to be relevant to Africans and therefore needs to be decolonised. In order to decolonise psychology we need to value and include uBuntu principles in our practice. In this regard, we need to adjust therapy frames. As Johnson and Sandhu (2010) suggest, when working in multicultural or intercultural contexts we need to adapt treatment to suit our clientele.

I acknowledge the excellent work of scholars who have developed alternatives to Western psychotherapy that can work for African people such as Nefale and Van Dyk's Ubuntu Therapy and NTU Therapy. The aim of this research is to add to those studies.

To begin, I feel it is important to briefly describe my own spiritual orientation: I believe that human being are spirit beings that live in bodies that have souls. I also believe that whatever is in the spirit of a human being manifests itself in the soul and whatever is in the soul manifests itself in the behaviour (body or physically). Both NTU Therapy and Ubuntu Therapy emphasise the importance of spirituality when working with Africans. The spirituality element in psychotherapy is relatively taboo in Western psychology.

In the section that follows I suggest how psychotherapists can professionally incorporate uBuntu in their practice. I recommend uBuntu principles to be incorporated in psychotherapy. Such uBuntu values are: interdependence; which has intra-interdependence, interpersonal inter-connectedness and spiritual-interconnectedness as sub-sections. Other uBuntu values include respect, going the extra mile, spirituality, sharing, psychoeducation, flexibility, touch and rapport, gifts and bartering, caring, humility, selflessness, compassion, African time, advice giving, dignity, normalising. These are briefly discussed below.

It is important to be cognisant of the interdependent nature of most Africans when working with them. According to Dolamo (2013) the uBuntu ethic sees a person as a process of coming into existence in the reciprocal relatedness of individual and community where the community includes God and the living-dead. In my view, interdependence is three-fold involving intra-interdependence, interpersonal-interconnectedness and spiritual-interconnectedness.

Intra-interdependence refers to the connection between the spirit, soul and body within oneself. In other words, one needs to be in touch with oneself and ensure wellness of the physical being, the soul and the spirit. One needs wellness in all three elements and psychotherapy may need to strive to achieve healthy connections between these three. Regarding interpersonal-interconnectedness, according to the literature it is important for Africans to interconnect with family and community as one is not perceived as an individual but rather as part of a bigger social unit. Family and society are very important. For example, in making decisions an African considers others instead of making decisions that will be beneficial to the individual only.

In the case of spiritual-interconnectedness, research has shown that Africans value spirituality more than other elements of life. This can be seen in the relationships and time spent with the living dead or ancestral worship or in the relationships with Christ/God. Most Africans view their successes or failures as the reward or reinforcement of certain behaviours either from God or ancestors. Ignoring such an important part of African living in psychotherapy may result in clients perceiving as the psychotherapist as lacking Spiritual Intelligence/Quotient (SQ). Dolamo (2013) noted that culture and religion are major pillars of uBuntu in Africa. Religion or spirituality has been proven to be a crucial part of African lives; I recommend that it not be ignored as part of the intervention when dealing with amaXhosa clients. However, because people have different spiritual beliefs, imposing the therapist's beliefs on the clients must be discouraged. All the forms of interconnectedness discussed above need to be foregrounded when working with African clients.

Respect is another key principle in psychotherapy in general, but has some additional aspects for consideration when working with African people. I recommend that respect is practised the African way when working with amaXhosa. Examples of African respect include not calling older people by their first names but rather using the relevant prefix such as Mr. Unconditional positive regard is also important in situations of impoverished economic status that is common in Black South African families. Respecting people because they are people and not respecting the 'haves' (affluent) more than the 'have nots' (poor) is an uBuntu value.

It is important to make psychotherapy work by respecting different people's unique situations. For example, where there is a need for collateral information from someone who cannot come to the office of a psychotherapist, the psychotherapist could go to the person. The most economical and respectful way of getting this collateral information is for the therapist to go to the home of the child client to interview the parents. It is a form of respect to go to the person instead of calling them to come to you, particularly if they are older in age.

Going the extra mile to assist an umXhosa client is an important therapy frame. It shows that one cares, wants to help and 'feels the pain' of the next person. This study therefore recommends that psychotherapists go the extra mile helping a client when they work with amaXhosa by, for example, phoning or sending an email to book an appointment for them in the doctor's rooms or finding out what time an institution closes they need to visit. Going the extra mile could facilitate healing and bring hope to clients.

I further recommend that sharing of information, ideas, tools to empower people such as books, is part of psychotherapy. This could be done in the form of psychoeducation. This could assist in educating people about how psychological services work in order to minimise confusion with the functions of medical practitioners or traditional healers, among others. This sharing of information through the use of psychoeducation could encourage amaXhosa males to consult more. Awareness campaigns and advocacy could be used to make more Africans aware of mental health issues, which could in turn assist in the expectations of clients for the outcomes of psychotherapy.

As much as sharing is part of uBuntu and I recommend that it not be limited to information but anything that could empower a fellow human being, I also recommend that psychotherapists be cognisant of not encouraging dependency from clients.

I recommend that HPCSA and other related professional bodies allow psychotherapists to use their discretion to practise in a culturally sensitive manner without fear of being judged or punished. Psychotherapists are trained and qualified to practice, they should be trusted as professionals.

To greet by hugging and by shaking of hands could be part of establishing rapport. Touching an African client in this sense is likely to be interpreted as a psychotherapist being friendly with the client and accepting the client as a person and is recommended. Since hugs and hand-shakes are common practices in uBuntu settings, I recommend that this become an accepted part of interacting with people in psychotherapy. However, this should be appropriate touching and must be comfortable to both the client and the therapist. It must never be sexual in any way.

As part of amaXhosa way of living, gifts and bartering in psychotherapy sessions, whether allowed by the professional body or not, is already taking place. In order for such actions to be appropriately regulated, I recommend they be allowed with conditions to avoid exploitation of either party. Bartering, to make psychotherapy sessions more accessible to poorer clients, can be in the form of a service or any other goods but regulating such exchange needs much greater debate by the profession.

These attributes seem to be important when working with amaXhosa as these are uBuntu values that seem helpful. Psychologists are perceived as being professional when they show they care for the client's situation and are compassionate about their experiences and this could facilitate their healing. I therefore recommend that psychotherapists show their clients that they care through incorporating uBuntu values in their practice. I also recommend humility when dealing with African clients and sharing helpful information with their clients and showing compassion when necessary. Display of these uBuntu values may facilitate healing for clients.

African time is common in African settings. For example, at a wedding it is expected that a bride must be late. Any ceremony starting at 09h00 will start much later and this is a phenomenon that is understood and accepted. This will always have a way of manifesting itself in some way. Ignoring the effect of this phenomenon in psychotherapy sessions could lead to misunderstandings between the client and psychotherapist which is not helpful in the therapy relationship. I recommend that psychotherapists use their discretion to deal with this issue.

Giving advice to the young or people that are not in the same field is a common practice among Africans. Clients might ask questions such as *ucebis'ukuba ndithini kule meko?* ('what do you advise me to do in this situation?') and it is awkward in a session if a psychotherapist refuses to advise. I recommend that it is accepted that in some cases people need advice from their psychotherapists and should be given it.

Isidima (dignity) is one of the values of uBuntu. For one to be respected one needs to display integrity, reliability and so on. According to Dolamo (2013) uBuntu has much to do with the integrity and dignity of an individual, which is both intrinsic and extrinsic. The latter means the person lives a dignified life while the former means the person has the will power to motivate themselves. Moreover, dignity of the person can be enhanced of diminished by the way an individual behaves within the community. Psychotherapy could assist in keeping one's dignity intact or restoring what has been lost.

Normalising has been used in psychotherapy and is a crucial therapy frame something I recommend is used if it can assist a client. If a particular personal experience could assist a client, I recommend that this be shared; however, a psychotherapist's experiences should not be the centre of the session.

In the light of what has been discussed above, I recommend a new African Psychology framework that could work for African clients, called an uBuntu-Centred Psychotherapy. This approach is derived from the data and literature in this study.

6.3 An uBuntu-Centred Psychotherapy

With regard to university training, learning should be contextualised such that it is relevant for the people concerned. The majority of people living in South Africa are Africans (Black) but psychology curricula in most universities are Eurocentric and there are very few lessons (if any) on African psychology or related topics. In order to contextualise psychology in South Africa, I recommend that African Psychology be a compulsory part of the curriculum. This approach believes that psychotherapy will always have certain elements of the West because psychology was born in the West. This approach also acknowledges that psychotherapy works for African people to a certain extent. It believes that the Western people and the African people are socialised differently and therefore have different values. It has its cornerstone as the values of uBuntu. It further perceives humans holistically as inspired by Dolamo (2013) who suggested that the African view is holistic in its approach towards the human person. It further believes that a human being is a spirit living in the body which possesses a soul.

This uBuntu-Centred Psychotherapy is premised on 'Healing the soul of African people using the soul of African society – *umntu ngumntu ngabantu'*. Characteristics of an uBuntu-Centred Psychotherapist and therapy sessions are discussed below.

6.3.1 Characteristics of uBuntu-Centred Psychotherapist

In uBuntu-Centred psychotherapy, psychotherapists view themselves as humans that are humane. They are people who live among other people, who are approachable anywhere. They assist in and out of their professional spaces. They acknowledge that although they may be experts in their field, they need others in other areas of their lives as well. According to Speight and Cadaret (cited in Leach & Welfel, 2018), culturally competent psychotherapists get themselves involved with community events, celebrations, and are neighbours. In other words, *bangabantu* (they are human). They are flexible, caring, humble, selfless and compassionate. They should be approachable; people should not fear them because they cannot talk to certain people in certain spaces. However, privacy and confidentiality of clients must be respected. They understand the history and cultural diversity background of South Africa. They are confident and acknowledge that most Africans have a poor socio-economic history that has impacted negatively on their lives, even after 25 years of democracy. The uBuntu -Centred psychotherapist keeps an open mind regarding languages spoken and cultural practices of different people in the South African rainbow nation. Leach and Horne (cited in Leach & Welfel, 2018) noted that cultural and linguistic variables add layers of complexity that have to be considered when working with people.

uBuntu -Centred psychotherapists are aware of gender issues. They are aware and respectful of African traditions such as amaXhosa traditions. Leach and Horne (cited in Leach & Welfel 2018) noted that cultural competence is an ethical imperative which requires psychotherapists have cultural knowledge. They also need to be aware of their own positionality in order to apply their skill sets appropriately to meet the needs of their clients.

All psychotherapists need to keep their integrity by doing the right thing even when no one seems to be watching (Welfel & Leach, 2018). They need to treat each client to the best of their abilities as if this was their only client.

6.3.2 uBuntu -centred psychotherapy sessions

uBuntu -Centred Psychotherapy sessions have the same basic structure as those in Eurocentric models of psychotherapy with a few added recommendations that are relevant to African clients.

6.3.2.1 Establishing rapport

I recommend that the psychotherapists consider applying uBuntu-Centred Psychotherapy ethical principles when working with African clients. This could be observed by greeting the client showing warmth by shaking hands or by hugging, if both the client and the psychotherapist are comfortable with touch. This could be used as a way of establishing rapport. To welcome the client, I recommend that a psychotherapist offer at least something to drink. Like hugs and handshakes, this offering of refreshment could be part of establishing rapport. It is interpreted as a sign of welcoming and accepting a person.

6.3.2.2 Psychoeducation

Another element of establishing rapport is psycho-education. This is important in order to clarify elements of confusion with a client that may be unfamiliar with psychotherapy. This psychoeducation could be limited to how psychological sessions work. In this regard, Vera and Speight (2003) noted that psycho-educational interventions should be prioritised in multi-culturally competent practices.

6.3.3 An uBuntu-Centred Psychotherapy model

The figure below depicts graphically the elements that could contribute to an effective uBuntu-Centred Psychotherapy model.

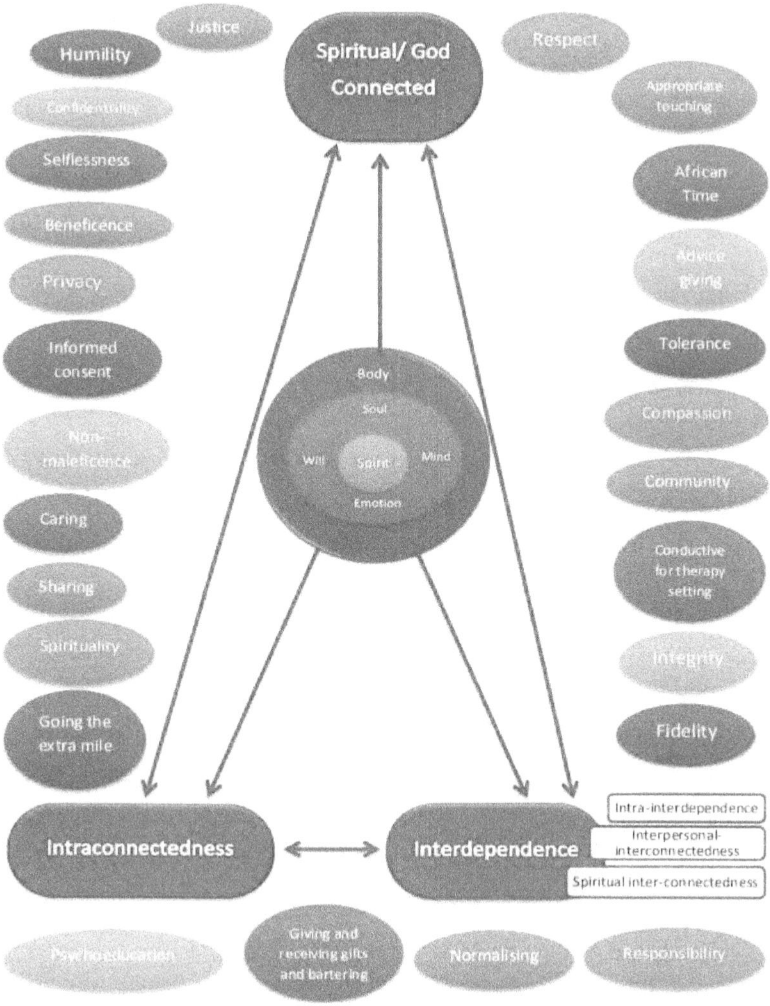

Figure 6.2: uBuntu-Centred Psychotherapy model

This model illustrates that uBuntu-Centred Psychotherapy believes that a human being is a spirit living in a body with a soul, foregrounding knowledge that an African individual is interdependent in these three facets of the self. An individual is intra-connected with the self; spirit, body and soul are intra-independent/connected. An individual is also interconnected with other humans – this is interdependence – and the interconnection with God is spiritual-interconnectedness. In figure 6.2 various ethics are shown indicating that a psychotherapist may pick whatever is relevant as needed. These uBuntu-Centred Psychotherapy ethical values and therapy frames have already been discussed and therefore will not be discussed in this section.

The uBuntu related principles pertinent to this approach are discussed in the section below.

6.3.4 Elements to be mindful of in uBuntu-Centred Psychotherapy

As psychotherapy sessions progress, the psychotherapist needs to acknowledge that an individual is interdependent: intra-interdependently, interpersonally-interconnected and spiritually-interconnected with the self, socially and with God. In this regard, Leach and Horne (cited in Leach & Welfel, 2018) noted that cultural competence requires a holistic appraisal of the person and their environment and the ability to design a range of interventions to address the needs of the clients.

6.3.4.1 Spirituality

Spirituality forms a big part of uBuntu or of the African way of living. African people mostly worship or believe in some power and perform rituals to worship that power. Participants sometimes encouraged clients to engage with isiXhosa traditions to deal with their challenges according to their beliefs. For example to help a particular client dealing with grief it was suggested that the client go to the grave of the loved one as the client believed that the deceased could hear him. Another example is of the psychotherapist encouraging the client to use prayer or *isiwasho* (cleansing water) to cleans himself of evil spirits and use salt to sprinkle in his house to chase away evil spirits or *impepho*(cleansing branch) to chase away evil spirits. amaXhosa clients must be supported and encouraged to practice what they believe in. Even when people move to urban areas they take their beliefs with them. A psychotherapist that ignores the local spiritual interpretation of a client ignores the soul of the indigenous community because Africans' natural, interpersonal, social, ecological and spiritual relationships are crucial to them (Mbiti, 1991). Africans often have spirituality and religion as the foundation of everything in their lives, for example, most ceremonies start and end with a prayer. Understanding and supporting the spirituality of people, I call spiritual competence of the psychotherapist or Spiritual Intelligence (SQ).

6.3.5 Principles of uBuntu-Centred Psychotherapy

uBuntu-Centred Psychotherapy ethics have their cornerstone as love. When one looks closely at uBuntu, it is about love. I believe that these principles could easily be observed when a psychotherapist authentically loves people as people and not as subjects.

Welfel and Leach (2018) indicated that psychotherapists are concerned about whether they will take an action that harms the client or ends treatment, because they want to do what is right. Applying the following principles of uBuntu-Centred Psychotherapy should be implemented without feeling guilty or having feelings of dissonance as long as there is no harm done in the process to either the client or the psychotherapist. Furthermore, whatever takes place must be in the best interest of the client.

Respect is another key element of the therapy frame and in uBuntu-Centred Psychotherapy certain traditional issues need to be observed. For example, if the client is an elderly female she should be called by her clan name such as *mamu'Madlamini* (mother Madlamini), a male should be called *tat'uNgconde* (father Ngconde). Other signs of respect must be displayed such as offering *isihlalo* (chair) then *impilo* (asking how they are doing) to show interest and respect. In the case where the clan name is unknown, one could be called by the surname but with a prefix such as *mam'u*Sidima (mother Sidima). This is a sign of respecting the dignity of a person. Differences also need to be respected.

Sharing is another amended therapy frame in uBuntu-Centred Psychotherapy – at times psychotherapists may need to share information or certain resources with the needy. This sharing of information could be done as part of psychoeducation. This includes giving advice to clients when advice is required but thorough information that may lead to the informed decision should be offered before giving advice. Giving of gifts and the receiving of gifts from clients also needs to be an acceptable part of therapy. However, I recommend this be regulated by the profession.

Other principles of uBuntu-Centred Psychotherapy include going the extra mile, normalising, African time, advice giving, and dignity. These have been discussed in detail and are only briefly outlined below as part of the uBuntu-Centred Psychotherapy model.

An uBuntu-Centred Psychotherapy ethic of going the extra mile is displayed by the psychotherapist who goes out of her way to ensure that the client is fully assisted. This is similar to the principle of beneficence where the therapist does his best to act in the best interest of the client. This includes looking for forms and helping clients fill these in – for an illiterate client assisting with filling in forms is going the extra mile.

Another uBuntu-Centred Psychotherapy ethic is normalising. This is done by referring to personal experiences, experiences of others, stories in the books, celebrities among others. Normalising mental illness in certain situations could be helpful and facilitate coping. Moreover, in cases of grief, normalising emotions that seem abnormal could be helpful.

African time is a reality when working with clients of African origin. uBuntu -Centred Psychotherapists are aware of this reality. They need to be flexible in dealing with this and use their discretion with each client.

uBuntu -Centred Psychotherapists give advice to clients; however discussions around the advice with the client are crucial. Advice should be given according to the needs of the client. Such advice can be part of encouraging the client towards achieving the goals of therapy.

It is crucial that the dignity of both the client and the psychotherapist are retained. I do not believe that therapy can be successful where the dignity of either party is affected. In such cases referral to another psychotherapist is recommended.

To draw the abovementioned ideas together, these are ethics that could be added to the existing HPCSA guidelines in order to accommodate people of African origin in psychotherapy. Incorporating these ethical principles could alleviate some of the feelings of dissonance among amaXhosa psychotherapists when working with clients of African origin and could result in positive psychotherapy outcomes. Moreover, fears of amaXhosa psychotherapists could be alleviated if HPCSA made uBuntu-Centred Psychotherapy ethical principles official.

6.5 Conclusion

It seems timely to make contributions in the psychology field that will embrace all contextual cultural perspectives of South Africa's rainbow nation. In this regard, Welfel and Leach (2018) suggested that charitable attributions with the fundamental values of the profession are needed. Maintaining ethical standards is crucial but not at the expense of the healing of a client, as advocated by beneficence and non-maleficence. Welfel and Leach (2018) suggested that it is important to know which ethical standards are required but other issues such as cultural background of a client should be considered by the psychotherapist. Participants in this study noted that the absence of a conscious acknowledgement of the reality of such concerns increases the risk of making the very ethical errors the practitioner wants to avoid and can lead psychotherapists to be reluctant to seek consultation or supervision. The findings of my study have led to the development of some uBuntu ethical principles that could be useful in psychotherapy when working with amaXhosa clients.

uBuntu-Centred Psychotherapy is not without faults, however I perceive it as a modality that can be implemented when working with clients of African origin and I feel that it could be improved with time and experience to become even more useful and relevant.

CHAPTER 7

CONCLUSION

The aim of this study is to provide and/or contribute knowledge in the field of psychotherapy concerning the psychotherapists' experiences regarding the incorporating principles of uBuntu in their practice. The idea of this study came about my professional experiences in my practice which led me into embarking on the journey to make sense of what made me frustrated, uncertain or caused dissonance in me about the way I practised. In other words, what made me want to justify certain actions I took when clients indicated that they have been helped and what made me feel so sad when I have practised the way 'I should' when I observe clients feeling failed in the sessions.

I will start by discussing my personal reflection on completion of the study, then I deliberate on practical implications of the study, I follow by describing the strengths and limitations of this study and finalise this chapter by making recommendations for future research projects.

7.1 Personal reflection on completion of the study

In most of the literature and research I have engaged with while doing this study, I found that researchers write about psychological principles that are embedded with Western principles. Some researchers of African origin write about feeling isolated by the profession particularly those that practice psychotherapy on African people. This reflected a gap that existed in the psychotherapy; which was highlighted by my personal experiences.

After my proposal on embarking on this journey was accepted I had to identify a population where I was to sample my participants. I then identified other psychologists in the area where I practise who are Black and have been in practise for five years or more, among amaXhosa as clients. Even before I interviewed my participants, I had to read about this and searched for a common frame of amaXhosa, I came up with the conceptual framework of uBuntu which was a way of living of Africans. In this I was inspired by African scholars, writers, freedom fighters such as tata Nelson Mandela, Steve Biko, Prof Nhlanhla Mkize and the like. For example, tata Mandela defined uBuntu as indicated in figure 7.1.

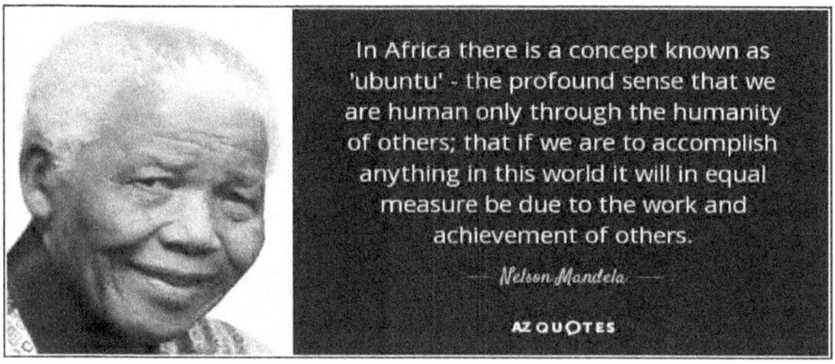

Figure 7.1: uBuntu definition by tata Nelson Mandela from a conversation with Richard Stengel, 29 April 1993

This means no person is an island and that achievements of people are obtained through the intervention of others. This is a core value of interdependence for people of African origin. This core value of uBuntu seems to contradict with the professional training during my time at the university.

This study made me realise that psychotherapy was not designed to service an African person but it was designed for the WEIRD. Be that as it may it came with the colonisers in Africa and it has been practised with Africans using the original principles and that is one of the reasons psychotherapy is not a perfect fit for Africans. Moreover, SA has a history of apartheid where Eurocentric ideas were practised and enforced on all peoples. Psychology formed part of those ideologies that were accepted without being questioned. The dilemmas and dissonances psychotherapists were experiencing mostly came from this. I understand that the ethical principles from HPCSA are binding for professionals, failing which one will be punished. However, therapy frames are not as rigid as the ethical principles and they can be altered to fit a particular context.

It is during the post #fees must fall protests era that decolonisation of apartheid or Eurocentric influenced practises became more actively interrogated and changed to be context relevant. Identifying and developing culturally appropriate psychological avenues for clinical practice for practitioners who work with indigenous people is timely and relevant (Kilcullen, Swinbourne & Cadet-James, 2018; Barnes & Siswana, 2018). By embarking on this study I intended to contribute knowledge within which a partially decolonised framework of psychotherapy was to be suggested. I aimed to come up with a theory or model that would be inclusive of uBuntu as the core value of Africans; which was excluded in the Eurocentric modalities. Welfel and Leach (2018) note that ethics education must have three goals: to reduce misconduct to the fullest extent possible; to motivate mental health professionals to commit to the profession's ethical values and principles, and to offer guidance about what to do next when we fall short of that goal. I therefore think uBuntu-Centred Psychotherapy is a modality that works for African people particularly amaXhosa because it is embedded with African principles. uBuntu -Centred principles reduce misconduct, motivate positive mental health and mean that African practitioners practice uBuntu naturally.

I also had initial difficulties to recruit a sample since I could not get willing participants for my study. This is due to the nature of this study. Psychotherapists did not want to see themselves being interrogated by the HPCSA due to malpractice because they included uBuntu in their practice, which is not part of the current ethical principles. In other words, practitioners are fearful to talk about such ethical issues because if they do not comply with the existing ethical codes, they feared they could be sanctioned in some way instead of being supported. The fact that they are not willing to be open about it, does not mean they do not do it.

This study gave me confidence in my practice. Before embarking on this study, the way I practised did not include this crucial and core element of the people I practised with and therefore it did not talk to them. I found myself torn between my way of living and my professional training. I used to be apologetic and have long explanations convincing myself and others why I gave that advice, or why I went out my way to assist the client, it felt that I was doing the right thing. I focused on practising correctly and congruently with what I was trained to do, complying with the principles instead of foregrounding the healing of my clients. Currently, I work with confidence as long as the client is assisted and no harm is done in the process, while I incorporate some uBuntu-Centred Psychotherapy principles. This is a work in progress, as Welfel and Leach (2018) indicate that culturally relevant psychotherapy ethics could be developed and improved with time and that that ethics education is a process and not an event.

During the data collection process, I interviewed participants on their experiences. The interview guide was designed based on my professional experiences. I interviewed eight psychologists who practised psychotherapy, who were isiXhosa speakers practising among amaXhosa clients and who were registered with HPCSA. These interviews mostly took place in the offices of psychotherapists. This means that my participants were on the ground, practising and these experiences they shared are exactly what needs to inform the profession. They have been trained in Eurocentric principles; they have witnessed these not working in all cases and have come up with ways that worked for their clients. So they know what works and what does not work for African clients.

However, uBuntu has been influenced by certain elements such as moral decay; and this means that it is not a unitary approach, or necessarily always foregrounded in people's modern interactions. I realise that there will be variations in practice due to different views on uBuntu, as a result it has evolved and changed from its original sense to suit our current style of living.

This study has also given me confidence to deal with all three facets of a human being in psychotherapy, namely the spirit, soul and body. I have gained more confidence in exploring the spirituality of clients, which is sometimes more important to Africans. This made me respect certain beliefs of people even more. Nwoye (2015) centralises spirituality much more in the psychotherapy room rather than in some Western models that view such topics as inappropriate. Inclusion of spirituality is a holistic approach in which spirituality is used as and when appropriate or raised by a client in a therapy session.

7.2 Practical implications of the study

This study has directed my steps towards coming up with a new model that could work when working with clients of African origin, particularly amaXhosa, called uBuntu-Centred Psychotherapy. This model is an attempt to bridge the gap that exists between the Eurocentric and uBuntu modalities needed practically to deal with multicultural practises. These may have practical implications for training and this its application will need to be explored.

This model then needs to be disseminated in order for other psychotherapists to utilise it in their practice. In order for this to be properly broadcasted, it needs relevant platforms such as the counselling psychology division of PsySSA, where a national conversation about these findings and this model will be further proposed. These discussions will be about what is needed practically in the field of psychotherapy. The APA encourages multicultural competencies and sensitivities. However, SA ethical codes are silent about these multicultural issues and these ethical codes are still widely influenced by the Western cultural perspectives. Ethical codes should be linked to these multicultural competences instead of becoming silent about such. Findings of this study could also be discussed with SAADCHE which is the association of student counsellors.

There are no models of ethical decision making that have been directly customised for the SA context. There is a need for such relevant models to SA context to be developed and be fed into the CPD. Leach (2012) suggests that it is good to attend CPD sessions because it is a requirement, however it is questionable whether those ethics emphasised in the CPD sessions will be implemented in practise. It is fine to make ethical training mandatory but practising using those Eurocentric ethical codes for African clients may not work. This means even though the intention of enforcing attendance of CPD sessions is positive, it does not encourage psychotherapists of African origin to utilise those Eurocentric principles, because they sometimes are not directly applicable. Some African psychotherapists attend those CPD training just to comply and to earn CPD points so that they are not in trouble with HPCSA.

Because this study seems to challenge the core of the current status of psychotherapy and due to fears of people of being punished should they be found practising in a way that is 'unacceptable' by HPCSA, psychotherapists are scared to discuss such issues in formal platforms. Psychotherapists of African origin due to their experience, know what works for their clients and no laws from HPCSA will stop them from doing what is right for their people but they will experience dilemmas as a result. This study is therefore opening up the space so that people particularly the most affected are less scared to talk about such issues. To discuss such issues openly may bring better solutions for psychotherapists to make informed decisions that are beneficial to the people they are servicing without fearing sanctions. As a profession we need to use supervision in a more open way so that people are not only fearful of punishment but can talk about the ethical dilemmas openly.

There is a lot talking about ethical codes, and there are no models in South Africa to inform ethical decisions, these need to be expanded. This study opens up a platform for such discussions.

7.3 Strengths and limitations of research

In this section I will start by discussing the strengths and then limitations of this research project.

7.3.1 Strengths

This study makes original contributions to the field of psychotherapy or counselling and psychology at large, in that uBuntu-Centred Psychotherapy is informed by the insiders. In other words, this study started from the field or based upon practical experiences rather than theoretical background. It is grounded on what people on the ground experience in their practice.

This study is conducted among the second biggest ethnic group in the country called amaXhosa, the biggest being the amaZulu. This study is certainly contributing towards Africanising Psychology. Although this debate on Africanising psychology has been present for the past few years there has not been much literature published about such. It contributes knowledge to African psychology where there is a limited literature.

This study has talked about tricky issues that people find it difficult to talk about although they are important issues. This is reflected in experiencing difficulties in finding psychologists that were willing to participate in this study. Those that eventually agreed to participate made sure that they were anonymous and that their contribution to this study was not going to bring trouble for them.

Phenomenology emphasises focusing on the experience of people that are in the field. So this study is not grounded on the imaginary issues or observations but it is based on their lived experiences as the IPA advocates. The pilot study conducted by me and my supervisor assisted in me bracketing my personal experiences.

"The professional rules of psychologists provide that it is inappropriate for psychologists to accept gifts from clients" Allan (2011:191). This study has proven that such statements are not applicable across the board. Psychologists have alluded to the fact that they have given and accepted gifts to and from clients; and no harm was done by such instead it helped in most cases. Such practices can be openly discussed by the profession.

This study is conducted by an insider, taking an insider's advantage of doing research. Although IPA talks about bracketing one's experiences I feel I obtained rich data from participants because I am an insider. Being an insider was also beneficial to me as a researcher in terms of collating data and making sense of data. Some of my participants' experiences resonated well with my own and that assisted me to probe and obtain rich data. I believe that participants shared more experiences because I was an insider and if I assured them that they will not be punished by sharing information about their experiences with me, then they trusted my word. However, I still feel that not everything they do was disclosed, for fearing to be judged or punished.

One of the strengths is my ability as a researcher to be bilingual and interchange between two languages as a South African. This has influenced the smooth flow in interviews where all my participants were also at least bilingual.

This study has therefore resulted in the birth of uBuntu-Centred Psychotherapy model. This modality suggests ways of practising psychotherapy that would assist psychotherapists to practice in an acceptable but effective manner without compromising people's ways of living, but also respecting the working rules and ethics of psychology. This model is supported by Allan (2011) by suggesting that harm can be unintentionally caused by using unproven or dangerous methods; by lacking foresight; by being incompetent; by being negligent and by failing to minimise or correct harm. Moreover, this modality can alleviate most of the dissonances experienced by psychotherapists because it is as much as it is rooted in uBuntu values, it also acknowledges some relevant Eurocentric ethical principles. This is reflective of the current way of living of South Africans, where the African worldviews and the Eurocentric perspectives are mostly combined.

7.3.2 Limitations

The sample size was informed by the methodology used in this study. Although it is a suggestion of the founders of IPA to have a smaller sample due to the in-depth analysis of data, the sample size is too small to generalise the findings. Only amaXhosa practising psychologists were sampled.

The study focused only on the sample of psychologists that practised in a small portion of the country and province. Only the semi-urban and urban psychologists were sampled, no rural ones contributed, although EC has a lot of rural settings.

Due to the fact that this study was about issues that people felt really uncomfortable to talk about because it had a potential of exposing them to being sanctioned by HPCSA should they not comply with the ethical codes, psychologists were reluctant to participate. This was my biggest challenge. Even those who participated wanted to be reassured that they were not to be reported to HPCSA.

The generalisability of this study, due to the sample size is a limitation but that will be for the next process in research. It is up to the others to see whether some of these ideas are not generalisable to other ethnic groups, to other language speakers, to other parts of the country.

Power relations were also a limitation. Although me and my participants were in the same profession and others were even more educated and had more practising experience that I had, because I was a researcher I had more power in this study. This could mean some people were doing some censoring of information.

Positivists would question the bias: that I am not objective enough, but that is a strength of a qualitative research. Bernard (2013) argues that bracketing our experiences helps us put our biases aside so that we do not view other people's experiences using our cultural lenses. This implies that the researcher has experiences about the topic being investigated.

The field of psychology even in SA is saturated by white practitioners. There are fewer Black practising psychologists compared to Whites but the country has the majority of Black people living in it. This then highlights the need to transform our practice to encourage more of the majority to join the profession, by creating approaches that resonate with them.

7.4 Recommendations for future research

This study was limited to the Eastern Cape Province of South Africa. I recommend that it can be done in other areas of SA. Moreover, since uBuntu has been shown in Chapter 3 to be an African concept, this study can be extended to all areas of Africa. A research topic could be around looking for ways of increasing Black practising psychotherapists in order for the majority of SA citizens to be serviced by people speaking their vernacular. It has been proven in the study that language is important in psychotherapy.

I recommend an expansion of sample size, to add more males in the sample as well as finding more information about the people that were reluctant to participate in this study and what caused them to be reluctant.

The CPD sessions need to be expanded to accommodate Africans as well particularly in SA, I do not think there is a psychotherapist that only sees whites in their practice, because that would be unconstitutional. Therefore because almost all practising psychotherapists do have African clients in their practice, uBuntu-Centred and similar modalities should be part of all the CPD sessions. I concur Amaeshi & Idemudia (2015) that African psychologists should start to develop theories, produce books with African pictures, examples of way of life, etc. These books should be recommended for schools. These can have attitudinal and motivational change for our students. Relying on books from the Western world limits our understanding of African psychology's understanding of disorders in general and consequently restricts the way we approach the way we approach treatment.

Although before this study I did not believe that there could be any intentional harm to participants, I became aware, during the interviews of the potentially sensitive material that was being shared with me, and some participants even asked for reassurances that they would not be reported to the HPCSA board for what they perceived as ethical infringements. This raises an issue for future research in this area, because it needs to be some sort of caveat that if any participants had reported practices that might be viewed in a serious light by the board, I may have been honour bound to inform them of these, to suggest they self-report such and to seek further supervision around the limits of confidentiality. However, disclosures that were made were of the nature that I considered them therapy frame issues, rather than actual ethical contraventions. In other words, no harm was done to clients nor psychotherapists.

I further recommend that university training for psychotherapists should include context relevant ethical principles. In such cases Leach and Welfel (2018) suggest to ethics educators to deepen and broaden ethics training beyond its current scope, could include discussing in training ethics courses. Moreover, these ethic courses tend to take place early in training. Vera and Speight (2003) recommend the infusion of multiculturalism into the curricula of training programmes in order to have students focused on teaching students to be culturally sensitive in therapeutic contexts. This could be a research topic to suggest how often ethics courses should be offered and the design of the course. I suggest that these uBuntu-Centred ethical principles be included in the university curriculums of psychotherapy. "Psychologists involved in the design of education and training programmes should be competent and should ensure that the programmes they develop will provide appropriate, current, accurate and representative knowledge and experience to students" Audi 1994 in Allan (2001:297).

Black females during the apartheid regime in SA were at the bottom of the hierarchy and that influenced them openly voicing their opinions on certain issues. I recommend that more African female voices be heard. Scholars such as Duncan, Van Niekerk, & Townsend (2004) as well as Seedat, et. al (2001) note the absence of Black and female voices in psychological writing. I recommend that research be done on how to encourage Black female psychotherapists to write more articles because they do have rich experiences that the profession could benefit from. In this regard Vera and Speight (2013) suggest that there is a need for macro level interventions when working with women and people of colour. I believe it is high time that the colour of psychology in SA becomes much more human and thus representative of the diverse people of SA. Another research topic could be in a form of debate on the popular newspapers where more ideas could be invited and debated on uBuntu and psychology. I further recommend different ways of collecting data such as using questionnaires, discussions and other methods of collecting data.

Myers, Joska, Lund, Levitt, Butler, Naledi, Milligan, Stein and Sorsdahl (2018) suggest a need for further mental health counselling within the context of chronic disease care in SA. They suggest a task-shared approach using lay counsellors to equip primary care workers with culture-appropriate counselling skills to reach out to more people in need. This could also be further explored as a research topic. I further recommend a study on how clients view the way psychotherapists of African origin practice.

Another research topic could be within the ethical code of conduct uBuntu should be further incorporated in psychology at large. A CPD programme could be made on uBuntu-Centred Psychotherapy. A committee where uBuntu related research projects are the focus could be established and research projects be made, just like what is taking place in the HIV/AIDS field. A research topic could include how this could take place. Formal suggestions need be made in this area of research, for candidates to embark on.

Another research topic could be on how to convince African males to make use of psychotherapy when a need arises. Awareness of psychological services, removing of stigma attached to psychological interventions could be a topic of research. A lot of research could be done nationally in SA to shift the people's views on constructions of male strength and competence. Psychology needs to be perceived as supportive and building strength rather that a service rendered to weak people. I believe that people are expressing themselves in road rages, substance abuse and criminal activities because they are not dealing with their challenges in a healthy manner.

7.5 Final comment

This research is based on the practical experiences of psychotherapists in their practice that are of African origin. I hope the contributions made in this study will be perceived by the profession with positive lenses for the development of the profession. I believe that this study has the potential to bring some transformation to the profession and to people that find it difficult to accept others. I further trust that the profession will evolve and become contextually relevant for South Africans. The uBuntu-Centred Psychotherapy although grounded in uBuntu values, it is mindful of relevant Western ethical principles reflective of the current South African context.

Printed in the USA
CPSIA information can be obtained
at www.ICGtesting.com
LVHW010430290824
789603LV00001B/118

9 798869 058959